# Fundamental of Financial Management

## :: Author ::

### Nilamben H. Sondarva

(M.COM.,B.ed., SLET)

## PUBLISHED BY

The New ERa International Publishing House

HQ. At & Po. Chaveli., Ta- Chansma,

Dist- Patan, North Gujarat, India, Asia.

www.iphouseindia.com

First Publication: 1st March, 2015

Copyright: Author
(c) Nilamben H. Sondarva

ISBN:- 978-15-08949-73-2

Price: Rs.750/- INDIA
$ 15 OUTSIDE INDIA

PUBLISHED BY

**The New ERa International Publishing House**
**HQ. At & Po. Chaveli., Ta- Chansma,**
**Dist- Patan, North Gujarat, India, Asia.**
**www.iphouseindia.com**

# Contents

# CHAPTER 1

# FINANCE FUNCTION & FINCIAL PLANNING

## Meaning of Financial Management

Financial Management means planning, organizing, directing and controlling the financial activities such as procurement and utilization of funds of the enterprise. It means applying general management principles to financial resources of the enterprise.

## Scope/Elements

1. Investment decisions includes investment in fixed assets (called as capital budgeting). Investment in current assets are also a part of investment decisions called as working capital decisions.

2. Financial decisions - They relate to the raising of finance from various resources which will depend upon decision on type of source, period of financing, cost of financing and the returns thereby.

3. Dividend decision - The finance manager has to take decision with regards to the net profit distribution. Net profits are generally divided into two:

   a. Dividend for shareholders- Dividend and the rate of it has to be decided.

b. Retained profits- Amount of retained profits has to be finalized which will depend upon expansion and diversification plans of the enterprise.

## Objectives of Financial Management

The financial management is generally concerned with procurement, allocation and control of financial resources of a concern. The objectives can be-

1. To ensure regular and adequate supply of funds to the concern.
2. To ensure adequate returns to the shareholders which will depend upon the earning capacity, market price of the share, expectations of the shareholders.
3. To ensure optimum funds utilization. Once the funds are procured, they should be utilized in maximum possible way at least cost.
4. To ensure safety on investment, i.e, funds should be invested in safe ventures so that adequate rate of return can be achieved.
5. To plan a sound capital structure-There should be sound and fair composition of capital so that a balance is maintained between debt and equity capital.

## Functions of Financial Management

1. **Estimation of capital requirements:** A finance manager has to make estimation with regards to capital requirements

of the company. This will depend upon expected costs and profits and future programmes and policies of a concern. Estimations have to be made in an adequate manner which increases earning capacity of enterprise.

2. **Determination of capital composition:** Once the estimation have been made, the capital structure have to be decided. This involves short- term and long- term debt equity analysis. This will depend upon the proportion of equity capital a company is possessing and additional funds which have to be raised from outside parties.

3. **Choice of sources of funds:** For additional funds to be procured, a company has many choices like-
   a. Issue of shares and debentures
   b. Loans to be taken from banks and financial institutions
   c. Public deposits to be drawn like in form of bonds.

Choice of factor will depend on relative merits and demerits of each source and period of financing.

4. **Investment of funds:** The finance manager has to decide to allocate funds into profitable ventures so that there is safety on investment and regular returns is possible.

5. **Disposal of surplus:** The net profits decision have to be made by the finance manager. This can be done in two ways:
   a. Dividend declaration - It includes identifying the rate of dividends and other benefits like bonus.

b. Retained profits - The volume has to be decided which will depend upon expansional, innovational, diversification plans of the company.

6. **Management of cash:** Finance manager has to make decisions with regards to cash management. Cash is required for many purposes like payment of wages and salaries, payment of electricity and water bills, payment to creditors, meeting current liabilities, maintainance of enough stock, purchase of raw materials, etc.

7. **Financial controls:** The finance manager has not only to plan, procure and utilize the funds but he also has to exercise control over finances. This can be done through many techniques like ratio analysis, financial forecasting, cost and profit control, etc.

## Meaning and Characteristics of Financial planning.

## Meaning and Characteristics of Financial planning.

Finance is the life blood of business. No business can run successfully without adequate finance. Finance is required to bring a business into existence, to keep it alive and also to see it growing and prospering.

### Meaning of Financial Planning:

Finance is an important function of business. The application of planning to this function is called financial planning. Financial planning is mainly concerned with the economical procurement and profitable use of funds. According to Gutlman and Dougall, "Financial planning is concerned with raising, controlling and administering of funds used in business." In the words of Bouneville and Dewey, "Financial planning consists in the raising, providing and managing of all the money, capital of funds of any kind to be used in connection with the business." Financial planning is an important element of the overall planning of business enterprise. Financial planning includes the following:

- Estimating the amount of capital required for financing the business enterprise;
- Determining capital structure;
- Laying down policies for the administration of capital;
- Formulating the programmes to provide the most effective use of capital.

**Characteristics of a Good/ Sound Financial Planning:**

The main characteristics of a good financial planning are as follows:

**Simplicity**

The financial plan should be as simple as possible so that it can be easily understood even by a layman, property executed and administered. A complicated financial plan creates unnecessary complications and confusion.

**Based on Clear-cut Objectives**

The financial plan should be based on the clear-cut objectives of the company. It should aim to procure adequate funds at the lowest cost so that the profitability of the business is improved.

## Flexibility

The financial plan should not be rigid, but rather flexible enough to accommodate the changes which may be introduced in it as and when necessary. The rigid composition of the financial plan may cause unnecessary irritation and may limit the future development of the business unit.

## Solvency an Liquidity

The financial plan should ensure solvency and liquidity of the business enterprise. solvency requires that short-term and long-term payments should be made on due dates positively. This will ensure credit worthiness and good will to the business enterprise. Liquidity means maintenance of adequate cash balance in hand. Sometimes insufficiency of cash may make a business enterprise bankrupt.

## Planning Foresight

Financial planning should have due foresight and vision to access the future needs, scope and scale of operation of the business enterprise. On the basis, financial planning should be done in such a manner that any adjustment needed in the future may be made without much difficulty. As the business proceeds, the financial adjustments become necessary which should be adjustable properly as and when desired.

## Contingencies Anticipated

The financial plan should be able to anticipate various contingencies which may arise in the near future. The financial plan should make adequate provision for meeting the challenge of unforeseen events.

## Minimum Dependence on Outside Sources

A long-term financial planning should aim at minimum dependence on outside resources. This can be possible by retaining a part of the profits for ploughing back.

## Intensive Use of Capital

Financial planning should ensure intensive use of capital. As far as possible, a proper balance between fixed and working capital should be maintained.

## Profitability

A financial plan should be drafted in such a way that the profitability of the business enterprise is not adversely affected.

## Economical

The financial plan should be quite economical i.e., the cost burden of raising various types of capital should be minimum.

## Government Financial Policy and Regulation

The financial policy should be prepared in accordance with the government financial policy and regulation. It should not violate it under any circumstances.

# The Role of the Finance Function in Organizational Processes

## The Finance Function and the Project Office

Contemporary organizations need to practice cost control if they are to survive the recessionary times. Given the fact that many top tier companies are currently mired in low growth and less activity situations, it is imperative that they control their costs as much as possible. This can happen only when the finance function in these companies is diligent and has a hawk eye towards the costs being incurred. Apart from this, companies also have to introduce efficiencies in the way their processes operate and this is another role for the finance function in modern day organizations.

Further, there must be synergies between the various processes and this is where the finance function can play a critical role. Lest one thinks that the finance function, which is essentially a support function, has to do this all by themselves, it is useful to note that, many contemporary organizations have dedicated project office teams for each division, which perform this function. In other words, whereas the finance function oversees the organizational processes at a macro level, the project office teams indulge in the same at the micro level.

This is the reason why finance and project budgeting and cost control have assumed significance because after all, companies exist to make profits and finance is the lifeblood that determines whether organizations are profitable or failures.

## The Pension Fund Management and Tax Activities of the Finance Function

The next role of the finance function is in payroll, claims processing, and acting as the repository of pension schemes and gratuity. If the US follow the 401(k) rule and the finance function manages the defined benefit and defined contribution schemes, in India it is the EPF or the Employee Provident Funds that are managed by the finance function. Of course, only large organizations have dedicated EPF trusts to take care of these aspects and the norm in most other organizations is to act as facilitators for the EPF scheme with the local or regional PF (Provident Fund) commissioner. The third aspect of the role of the finance function is to manage the taxes and their collection at source from the employees. Whereas in the US, TDS or Tax Deduction at Source works differently from other countries, in India and much of the Western world, it is mandatory for organizations to deduct tax at source from the employees commensurate with their pay and benefits. The finance function also has to coordinate with the tax authorities and hand out the annual tax statements that form the basis of the employee's tax returns. Often, this is a sensitive and critical process since the tax rules mandate very strict principles for generating the tax statements.

## Payroll, Claims Processing, and Automation

We have discussed the pension fund management and the tax deduction. The other role of the finance function is to process payroll and associated benefits in time and in tune with the regulatory requirements. Further, claims made by the employees with respect to medical, and transport allowances have to be processed by the finance function. Often, many organizations automate this routine activity wherein the use of ERP (Enterprise Resource Planning) software and financial workflow automation software make the job and the task of claims processing easier. Having said that, it must be remembered that the finance function has to do its due diligence on the claims being submitted to ensure that bogus claims and suspicious activities are found out and stopped. This is the reason why many organizations have experienced chartered accountants and financial professionals in charge of the finance function so that these aspects can be managed professionally and in a trustworthy manner.

The key aspect here is that the finance function must be headed by persons of high integrity and trust that the management reposes in them must not be misused. In conclusion, the finance function though a non-core process in many organizations has come to occupy a place of prominence

## Role of a Financial Manager

Financial activities of a firm is one of the most important and complex activities of a firm. Therefore in order to take care of these activities a financial manager performs all the requisite financial activities.

A financial manger is a person who takes care of all the important financial functions of an organization. The person in charge should maintain a far sightedness in order to ensure that the funds are utilized in the most efficient manner. His actions directly affect the Profitability, growth and goodwill of the firm.

### Following are the main functions of a Financial Manager:

### 1. Raising of Funds

In order to meet the obligation of the business it is important to have enough cash and liquidity. A firm can raise funds by the way of equity and debt. It is the responsibility of a financial manager to decide the ratio between debt and equity. It is important to maintain a good balance between equity and debt.

### 2. Allocation of Funds

Once the funds are raised through different channels the next important function is to allocate the funds. The funds should be allocated in such a manner that they are optimally used. In order to allocate funds in the best possible manner the following point must be considered

- The size of the firm and its growth capability
- Status of assets whether they are long term or short tem
- Mode by which the funds are raised.

These financial decisions directly and indirectly influence other managerial activities. Hence formation of a good asset mix and proper allocation of funds is one of the most important activity

## 3. Profit Planning

Profit earning is one of the prime functions of any business organization. Profit earning is important for survival and sustenance of any organization. Profit planning refers to proper usage of the profit generated by the firm. Profit arises due to many factors such as pricing, industry competition, state of the economy, mechanism of demand and supply, cost and output. A healthy mix of variable and fixed factors of production can lead to an increase in the profitability of the firm.

Fixed costs are incurred by the use of fixed factors of production such as land and machinery. In order to maintain a tandem it is important to continuously value the depreciation cost of fixed cost of production. An opportunity cost must be calculated in order to replace those factors of production which has gone thrown wear and tear. If this is not noted then these fixed cost can cause huge fluctuations in profit.

## 4. Understanding Capital Markets

Shares of a company are traded on stock exchange and

there is a continuous sale and purchase of securities. Hence a clear understanding of capital market is an important function of a financial manager. When securities are traded on stock market there involves a huge amount of risk involved.

Therefore a financial manger understands and calculates

the risk involved in this trading of shares and debentures. Its on the discretion of a financial manager as to how distribute the profits. Many investors do not like the firm to distribute the profits amongst share holders as dividend instead invest in the business itself to enhance growth. The practices of a financial manager directly impact the operation in capital market.

<u>**What are the goals of Financial Management?**</u>
**What are the goals of Financial Management?**

The financial management has to take three important decision viz. (i) Investment decision i.e., where to invest fund and in what amount, (ii) Financing decision i.e., from where to raise funds and in what amount, and (iii) Dividend i.e., how much to pay dividend and how much to retain for future expansion. In order to make these decisions the management must have a clear understanding of the objective sought to be achieved. It is generally agreed that the financial objective of the firm should be maximization of owner's economic welfare. There are two widely discussed approaches or criterion of maximizing owners' welfare -(i) Profit maximization, and (ii) Wealth maximization. It should be noted here that objective is used in the sense of goal or goals or decision criterion for the three decisions involved.

**Profit Maximization:** Maximization of profits is very often considered as the mainobjective of a business enterprise. The shareholders, the owners of the business, invest their funds in the business with the hope of getting higher dividend on their investment. Moreover, the profitability of the business is an indicator of the sound health of the organisation, because, it safeguards the economic interests of various social groups which are directly or indirectly connected with the company e.g. shareholders, creditors and employees. All these parties must get reasonable return for their contributions and it is possible only when company earns higher profits or sufficient profits to discharge the obligations to them.

**Wealth Maximization:** The wealth maximization (also known as value maximization or Net Present Worth Maximization) is also universally accepted criterion for financial decision making. The value of an asset should be viewed in terms of benefits it can produce over the cost of capital investment.

**Prof. Era Solomon** has defined the concept of wealth maximization as follows- "The gross present worth of a course of action is equal to the capitalized value of the flow of future expected benefits, discounted (or as capitalized) at a rate which reflects their certainty or uncertainty. Wealth or net amount of capital investment required to achieve the benefits being discussed. Any financial action which creates wealth or which has a net present worth above zero is a desirable one and should be undertaken. Any financial action which does not meet this test should be rejected.

If two or more desirable courses of action are mutually exclusive (i.e., if only one can be undertaken) then the decision should be to do that which creates most wealth or shows the greatest amount of net present worth. In short, the operating objective for financial management is to maximize wealth or net present worth. Thus, the concept of wealth maximization is based on cash flows (inflows and outflows) generated by the decision. If inflows are greater than outflows, the decision is good because it maximizes the wealth of the owners.

We have discussed above the two goals of financial management. Now the question is which one is the best or which goal should be followed in decision making. Certain objections have been raised against the profit maximization goal which strengthen the case for wealth maximization as the goal of financial decisions.

STAGES / PROCEDURE OF FINANCIAL PLANNING

**FINANCIAL PLANNING PROCESS**

The financial planning process consists of the following six steps:

1. **Establish and define the client-planner relationship.**

   The financial planner should clearly explain and document the services that he or she will provide to you and define both his/her and your responsibilities during the financial planning engagement. The financial planner should explain fully how he or she will be paid and by whom. You and the planner should agree on how long the professional relationship should last and on how decisions will be made.

2. **Gather client data, including goals.**

The financial planner should ask for information about your financial situation. You and the planner should mutually define your personal and financial goals, understand your time frame for results and discuss, if relevant, how you feel about risk. The financial planner should gather all the necessary documents before giving you the advice you need.

3. **Analyze and evaluate your financial status.**

The financial planner should analyze your information to assess your current situation and determine what you must do to meet your goals. Depending on what services you have asked for, this could include analyzing your assets, liabilities and cash flow, current insurance coverage, investments or tax strategies.

4. **Develop and present financial planning recommendations and/or alternatives.**

The financial planner should offer financial planning recommendations that address your goals, based on the information you provide. The planner should go over the recommendations with you to help you understand them so that you can make informed decisions. The planner should also listen to your concerns and revise the recommendations as appropriate.

5. **Implement the financial planning recommendations.**

You and the financial planner should agree on how the recommendations will be carried out. The planner may carry out the recommendations or serve as your coach, coordinating the process with you and other professionals such as attorneys, accountants or stockbrokers.

6. **Monitor the financial planning recommendations.**

You and the financial planner should agree on who will monitor your progress towards your goals. If the planner is in charge of the process, he or she should report to you periodically to review your situation and adjust the recommendations, if needed, as your life changes.

# CHAPTER 2.

# CAPITALIZATION & CAPITAL STRUCTURE

## CAPITALISATION :

### What is Capitalization

Capitalization comprises of share capital, debentures, loans, free reserves,etc. Capitalization represents permanent investment in companies excluding long-term loans. Capitalization can be distinguished from capital structure. Capital structure is a broad term and it deals with qualitative aspect of finance. While capitalization is a narrow term and it deals with the quantitative aspect.

Capitalization is generally found to be of following types-

- Normal
- Over
- Under

### Overcapitalization

Overcapitalization is a situation in which actual profits of a company are not sufficient enough to pay interest on debentures, on loans and pay dividends on shares over a period of time. This situation arises when the company raises more capital than required. A part of capital always remains idle. With a result, the rate of return shows a declining trend. The causes can be-

1. **High promotion cost-** When a company goes for high promotional expenditure, i.e., making contracts,

canvassing, underwriting commission, drafting of documents, etc. and the actual returns are not adequate in proportion to high expenses, the company is over-capitalized in such cases.

2. **Purchase of assets at higher prices-** When a company purchases assets at an inflated rate, the result is that the book value of assets is more than the actual returns. This situation gives rise to over-capitalization of company.

3. **A company's floatation n boom period-** At times company has to secure it's solvency and thereby float in boom periods. That is the time when rate of returns are less as compared to capital employed. This results in actual earnings lowering down and earnings per share declining.

4. **Inadequate provision for depreciation-** If the finance manager is unable to provide an adequate rate of depreciation, the result is that inadequate funds are available when the assets have to be replaced or when they become obsolete. New assets have to be purchased at high prices which prove to be expensive.

5. **Liberal dividend policy-** When the directors of a company liberally divide the dividends into the shareholders, the result is inadequate retained profits which are very essential for high earnings of the company. The result is deficiency in company. To fill up the deficiency, fresh capital is raised which proves to be a costlier affair and leaves the company to be over- capitalized.

6. **Over-estimation of earnings-** When the promoters of the company overestimate the earnings due to inadequate financial planning, the result is that company goes for borrowings which cannot be easily met and capital is not profitably invested. This results in consequent decrease in earnings per share.

## Effects of Overcapitalization

1. **On Shareholders-** The over capitalized companies have following disadvantages to shareholders:

   a. Since the profitability decreases, the rate of earning of shareholders also decreases.

   b. The market price of shares goes down because of low profitability.

   c. The profitability going down has an effect on the shareholders. Their earnings become uncertain.

   d. With the decline in goodwill of the company, share prices decline. As a result shares cannot be marketed in capital market.

2. **On Company-**

   a. Because of low profitability, reputation of company is lowered.

   b. The company's shares cannot be easily marketed.

   c. With the decline of earnings of company, goodwill of the company declines and the result is fresh borrowings are difficult to be made because of loss of credibility.

d. In order to retain the company's image, the company indulges in malpractices like manipulation of accounts to show high earnings.

e. The company cuts down it's expenditure on maintainance, replacement of assets, adequate depreciation, etc.

3. **On Public-** An overcapitalized company has got many adverse effects on the public:

a. In order to cover up their earning capacity, the management indulges in tactics like increase in prices or decrease in quality.

b. Return on capital employed is low. This gives an impression to the public that their financial resources are not utilized properly.

c. Low earnings of the company affects the credibility of the company as the company is not able to pay it's creditors on time.

d. It also has an effect on working conditions and payment of wages and salaries also lessen.

## Undercapitalization

An undercapitalized company is one which incurs exceptionally high profits as compared to industry. An undercapitalized company situation arises when the estimated earnings are very low as compared to actual profits. This gives rise to additional funds, additional profits, high goodwill, high earnings and thus the return on capital shows an increasing trend. The causes can be-

1. **Low promotion costs**
2. **Purchase of assets at deflated rates**
3. **Conservative dividend policy**
4. **Floatation of company in depression stage**
5. **High efficiency of directors**
6. **Adequate provision of depreciation**
7. **Large secret reserves are maintained.**

## Efffects of Under Capitalization

1. **On Shareholders**
   a. Company's profitability increases. As a result, rate of earnings go up.
   b. Market value of share rises.
   c. Financial reputation also increases.
   d. Shareholders can expect a high dividend.
2. **On company**
   a. With greater earnings, reputation becomes strong.
   b. Higher rate of earnings attract competition in market.
   c. Demand of workers may rise because of high profits.

d. The high profitability situation affects consumer interest as they think that the company is overcharging on products.

3. **On Society**

a. With high earnings, high profitability, high market price of shares, there can be unhealthy speculation in stock market.

b. 'Restlessness in general public is developed as they link high profits with high prices of product.

c. Secret reserves are maintained by the company which can result in paying lower taxes to government.

d. The general public inculcates high expectations of these companies as these companies can import innovations, high technology and thereby best quality of product.

## CAPITAL STRUCTURE :

### Meaning of Capital Structure

Capital Structure is referred to as the ratio of different kinds of securities raised by a firm as long-term finance. The capital structure involves two decisions-

a. Type of securities to be issued are equity shares, preference shares and long term borrowings (Debentures).

b. Relative ratio of securities can be determined by process of capital gearing. On this basis, the companies are divided into two-

i.  Highly geared companies - Those companies whose proportion of equity capitalization is small.

ii. Low geared companies - Those companies whose equity capital dominates total capitalization.

For instance - There are two companies A and B. Total capitalization amounts to be USD 200,000 in each case. The ratio of equity capital to total capitalization in company A is USD 50,000, while in company B, ratio of equity capital is USD 150,000 to total capitalization, i.e, in Company A, proportion is 25% and in company B, proportion is 75%. In such cases, company A is considered to be a highly geared company and company B is low geared company.

**Factors Determining Capital Structure**

1. **Trading on Equity-** The word "equity" denotes the ownership of the company. Trading on equity means taking advantage of equity share capital to borrowed funds on reasonable basis. It refers to additional profits that equity shareholders earn because of issuance of debentures and preference shares. It is based on the thought that if the rate of dividend on preference capital and the rate of interest on borrowed capital is lower than the general rate of company's earnings, equity shareholders are at advantage which means a company should go for a judicious blend of

preference shares, equity shares as well as debentures. Trading on equity becomes more important when expectations of shareholders are high.

2. **Degree of control-** In a company, it is the directors who are so called elected representatives of equity shareholders. These members have got maximum voting rights in a concern as compared to the preference shareholders and debenture holders. Preference shareholders have reasonably less voting rights while debenture holders have no voting rights. If the company's management policies are such that they want to retain their voting rights in their hands, the capital structure consists of debenture holders and loans rather than equity shares.

3. **Flexibility of financial plan-** In an enterprise, the capital structure should be such that there is both contractions as well as relaxation in plans. Debentures and loans can be refunded back as the time requires. While equity capital cannot be refunded at any point which provides rigidity to plans. Therefore, in order to make the capital structure possible, the company should go for issue of debentures and other loans.

4. **Choice of investors-** The company's policy generally is to have different categories of investors for securities. Therefore, a capital structure should give enough choice to all kind of investors to invest. Bold and adventurous investors generally go for equity shares and loans and

debentures are generally raised keeping into mind conscious investors.

5. **Capital market condition-** In the lifetime of the company, the market price of the shares has got an important influence. During the depression period, the company's capital structure generally consists of debentures and loans. While in period of boons and inflation, the company's capital should consist of share capital generally equity shares.

6. **Period of financing-** When company wants to raise finance for short period, it goes for loans from banks and other institutions; while for long period it goes for issue of shares and debentures.

7. **Cost of financing-** In a capital structure, the company has to look to the factor of cost when securities are raised. It is seen that debentures at the time of profit earning of company prove to be a cheaper source of finance as compared to equity shares where equity shareholders demand an extra share in profits.

8. **Stability of sales-** An established business which has a growing market and high sales turnover, the company is in position to meet fixed commitments. Interest on debentures has to be paid regardless of profit. Therefore, when sales are high, thereby the profits are high and company is in better position to meet such fixed commitments like interest on debentures and dividends on preference shares. If

company is having unstable sales, then the company is not in position to meet fixed obligations. So, equity capital proves to be safe in such cases.

9. **Sizes of a company-** Small size business firms capital structure generally consists of loans from banks and retained profits. While on the other hand, big companies having goodwill, stability and an established profit can easily go for issuance of shares and debentures as well as loans and borrowings from financial institutions. The bigger the size, the wider is total capitalization.

## What is Capital Structure?

Capital structure describes how a corporation finances its assets. This structure is usually a combination of several sources of senior debt, mezzanine debt and equity. Wise companies use the right combination of senior debt, mezzanine debt and equity to keep their true cost of capital as low as possible. Depending on how complex the structure, there may in fact be dozens of financing sources included, drawing on funds from a variety of entities in order to generate the complete financing package. Capital structure is what describes the relationship of these financing sources as they appear on the corporation's balance sheet.

Examples of capital sources that may be included in a corporation's capital structure are:

- <u>Working Capital</u>
- <u>Equity</u>
- <u>Senior Debt</u>
- <u>Mezzanine Debt</u>
- <u>Alternatives</u>

What is Working Capital (WC)?

Working Capital (WC) is calculated by subtracting a corporation's current liabilities from its current assets. This financial metric determines a corporation's operating liquidity and is necessary in understanding how readily available funds are for necessary financial transactions related to daily operations. A corporation whose current liabilities are more than its current assets is considered to have a working capital deficiency.

Working Capital (WC) is calculated as follows:

Working Capital = Current Assets - Current Liabilities

The danger of having negative working capital is that a corporation may be unable to meet its short-term liabilities. Examples of current assets are cash, accounts receivables and inventory. These assets are easily liquidated for the purpose of raising funds. If a corporation is unable to meet its short-term obligations, then in a worst case scenario, bankruptcy may be a threat. In addition, negative working capital may also be a sign of trouble ahead. If negative working capital remains over a long period of time, this may be an indication that sales volumes are on the decline.

What is Equity?

Equity describes the value of an ownership stake or interest in a property. When a corporation is initially established, owners contribute funds to help finance assets. In exchange for those funds, a liability is created on the corporation to its owners in the form of share capital. The capital that is formed is equity and it represents the sum of the investments made in a corporation - typically in exchange for shares. Equity is also known as risk capital or liable capital.

Shareholders' equity is the amount of funds that have been contributed by the owners of the corporation, plus any retained earnings that have accumulated. Losses incurred by the corporation will negatively affect shareholders equity since the losses are ultimately the responsibility of the owners. Equity is found on the corporations balance sheet and is an integral element of how a business's finances are managed and accounted for.

Because equity is inherently risky, equity investors are generally looking for at least a 25% return if not more which is fundamentally the reason why equity capital is considered the most expensive form of capital compared to mezzanine debt.

What is Senior Debt?

Senior debt is the first level of a corporation's liabilities which means it is paid out first, ahead of all other creditors. Senior debt, as opposed to junior debt, is first in seniority and is often secured by collateral in the form of a lien.

Senior debt is among the safest form of financing for the party providing the funds. Due to its inherent low risk, it also provides the least amount of return. However, in exchange for this low return, significant protection is provided even in the event of bankruptcy. Should a corporation go bankrupt, any remaining funds, dissolved assets or other available sources of value must first repay senior debt before other creditors are able to collect.

Senior debt is financing that has been lent to a corporation for a pre-negotiated period of time with interest paid on the principal. The lender profits from this arrangement due to the scheduled period of borrowing on which the interest applies. The risk is low, since the borrower is contractually obligated to make payments on a pre-determined schedule. The lender does not gain the benefit of a higher potential return since the financing and its recoupment is not based on the borrowers financial performance. For this reason, senior debt is prioritized over other investments and creditors.

## What do you Mean by Trading on Equity?

Trading on equity means to raise fixed cost capital (borrowed capital and preference share capital) on the basis of equity share capital so as to increasing the income of equity shareholders.

Although it is possible only when the rate of return of the company is greater than the rate of interest on borrowed capital or the rate of dividend on preference shares.

EBIT is that profit of the business from which the payment of interest and tax remains to be deducted. It is also known as the operating profit of business. This is an index of the profit earning capacity of the business.

For example, the EBIT in case of two companies is rupees eight crore and ten crore respectively while their EAIT (Earning after Interest and Taxes) is five crore and four crore respectively. Here, it can be said that on the basis of EBIT the second company has a more profit-earning capacity.

Those investors who provide fixed cost capital to the company have limited share in its (company's) profits (in the form of interest on borrowed capital and dividend on preference shares).

Hence, they want their investment to remain safe by owners' capital. In other words, lenders will be willing to give loan to the company only when the base of the company is strong, meaning thereby, when the company has sufficient equity share capital.

Lenders desire it to be so, because in case the company suffers heavy loss or goes bankrupt then equity shareholders alone will suffer. Because of priority payment to the lenders their loans will remain safe.

Now the question arises how the income (earning) of the equity shareholders can increase when the company raises fixed cost capital (borrowed capital). Following EBIT-EPS Analysis answers this question:

It is clear from the above table that both the companies have raised 10, 00,000 as total capital. But X Co. has raised it by issuing equity capital. On the other hand, Y Co. has risen 4, 00,000 by issuing equity capital and 6, 00,000 by issuing debentures bearing 10% fixed interest. Suppose, both the companies have earned EBIT lakh each and tax rate is 30%.

After the deduction of the Interest and Tax respectively out of EBIT, the balance left is known EAIT. It is also known as EAT (Earning after Tax) because the interest is paid before the payment of tax.

First of all preference dividend (if any) is deducted from EAT. In this way the amount available is called Earning

Available for Equity Shareholders. On this very basic EPS is found over or calculated.

## Leverage and Types of Leverages

Leverage is a practice which can help a business drive up its gains / losses. In business language, if a firm has fixed expenses in P/L account or debt in capital structure, the firm is said to be levered. Now-a-days, almost no business is away from leverage but very few have struck a balance.

## Leverage and Types of Leverages

In finance, leverage is very closely related to fixed expenses. We can safely state that by introduction of expenses which are fixed in nature, we are leveraging a firm. By fixed expenses, we refer to the expenses, the amount of which remains unchanged irrespective of the activity of the business. For example, amount of investment made in fixed assets or interest paid on loans does not change with a normal change in the amount of sales. Neither they decrease with decrease in sales and nor they increase with increase in sales.

There are different basis for classifying business expenses. For our convenience, let us classify fixed expenses into operating fixed expenses such as depreciation on fixed expenses, salaries etc, and financial fixed expenses such as interest and dividend on preference shares. Similar to them, leverages are also of two types – <u>financial leverage</u> and operating leverage.

**Financial Leverage:** Financial leverage is a leverage created with the help of debt component in the capital structure of a company. Higher the debt, higher would be the financial leverage because with higher debt comes the higher amount of interest that needs to be paid. Leverage can be both good and bad for a business depending on the situation. If a firm is able to generate a higher return on investment (ROI) than the interest rate it is paying, leverage will have its positive effect shareholder's return. The darker side is that if the said situation is opposite, higher leverage can take a business to a worst situation like bankruptcy.

**Operating Leverage:** Operating leverage, just like the financial leverage, is a result of operating fixed expenses. Higher the fixed expense, higher is the operating leverage. Like the financial leverage had an impact on the shareholder's return or say earnings per share, operating leverage directly impacts the operating profits (Profits before Interest and Taxes (PBIT)). Under good economic conditions, due to operating leverage, an increase of 1% in sales will have more than 1% change in operating profits.

# CHAPTER 3

# WORKING CAPITAL MANAGEMENT

## Meaning And Concept Of Working Capital
### *Meaning Of Working Capital*

Business organization require adequate capital to establish business and operate theiractivities. The total capital of a business can be classified as fixed capital and working capital. Fixed capital is required for thepurchase of fixed assets like building, land, machinery, furniture etc. Fixed capital is invested for long period, therefore it is known as long-term capital.Similarly, the capital, which is needed for investing in current assets, is called working capital.

The capital which is needed for the regular operation of business is called working capital. Working capital is also called circulating capital or revolving capital or short-term capital. Working capital is used for regular business activities like for the purchase of raw materials, for the payment of wages, payment of rent and of other expenses. Working capital is kept in the form of cash, debtors, raw materials inventory, stock of finished goods, bills receivable etc.

### *Concept Of Working Capital*

Generally, there are two concepts of working capital i.e. gross concept and net concept.

## 1. Gross Concept Of Working Capital

According to gross concept, working capital refers to all the current assets and represents the amount of funds invested in current assets. Thus, gross working capital is the capital invested in current assets. Current assets are those assets which can be converted into cash within the short-time period. *Gross Working Capital = Total current assets*

In this way, gross working capital refers to the firm's investment in current assets. Gross working capital represents total of current assets which includes cash in hand, cash at bank, inventory, prepaid expenses, bills receivable etc.

## 2. Net Concept Of Working Capital

According to the net concept, working capital is the excess of current assets over current liabilities. In other words, the difference between current assets and current liabilities is called net working capital.

*Net Working Capital = Current Assets - Current liabilities*
In this way, net working capital is the difference of current assets and current liabilities.

## Types of Working Capital

Working Capital is divided into various types based balance sheet view and operating cycle view. Balance sheet view divides working capital into gross working capital and <u>net working capital</u> and the operating cycle view divides the working capital into permanent and temporary working capital. Permanent working capital is further divided into seasonal and special working capital whereas temporary working capital into regular and reserve working capital.

## Types of Working Capital

Working capital is the capital / funds required for day to day operations of the business. Working capital is invested usually in all types of inventories such as raw materials, spares, finished goods etc and credit extension to debtors and cash in hand.

## Types of Working Capital:

Working capital is classified into different types and the classification is based on the following views:

1. Balance Sheet View
2. Operating Cycle View

**On the basis of Balance Sheet View, types of working capital are described below:**

- **Gross Working Capital (GWC):** Current assets in the balance sheet of a company are known as gross working capital. Current assets are those short term assets which can be converted into cash within a period of one year. The grey area in the management of current assets or gross working capital is its unpredictability i.e. it is very difficult to ascertain the exact time of conversion of such assets. Why such a nature is problematic? It is because the liabilities occur at their time and do not wait for our current asset to realize. This mismatch or the gap creates a need for arranging working capital financing.

- **Net Working Capital (NWC):** Net working capital is a very frequently used term. There are two ways to understand net working capital. First one says it is simply the difference of current assets and the current liabilities in the balance sheet of a business. The other understanding discloses little deeper or hidden meaning of the term. As per that, NWC is that part of current assets which are indirectly financed by long term assets. Compared to gross working capital, net working capital is considered more relevant for effective working capital financing and management.

***On the basis of Operating Cycle View, types of working capital are as below:***

- **Permanent / Fixed Working Capital:** Dealing with current asset and fixed assets is totally different. Determining the financing requirement in case of fixed assets is simply the cost of the asset. Same is not true for current assets because value of current assets is constantly changing and it is difficult to accurately forecast that value at any point of time. To simplify the complexity to some extent, on the basis of past trend and experience, we can find a level below which current asset has never gone. The current assets below this level are calledpermanent or fixed working capital. See the example below:

| Types of Working Capital | | |
| --- | --- | --- |
| Net Working Capital | Permanent / Fixed Working Capital | Temporary / Variable Working Capital Requirement |

| 3000 | 2500 | 500 |
| --- | --- | --- |
| 2500 | 2500 | 0 |
| 2800 | 2500 | 300 |
| 3200 | 2500 | 700 |

In the example, 2500 is the permanent working capital

below which the net working capital has not gone.

- *Regular Working Capital:* It is the permanent working capital which is normally required in the normal course of business for the working capital cycle to flow smoothly.
- *Reserve Working Capital:* It is the working capital available over and above regular working capital. It is kept for contingencies which may arise due to unexpected situations.

- **Temporary / Variable WC:**Temporary working capital is easy to understand after getting hold over permanent working capital. In simple terms, it is the difference between net working capital and permanent working capital. The main characteristic which can be made out from the example is "fluctuation". The temporary working capital therefore cannot be forecasted. In the interest of measurability, this can be further bifurcated as below which can create at least some base to forecast.

- ○ *Seasonal Working Capital:* Seasonal working capital is that temporary increase in working capital which is caused due to some relevant season for the business. It is applicable to businesses having impact of seasons for example, manufacturer of sweaters for whom relevant season is the winters. Normally, their working capital requirement would increase in that season due to higher sales in that period and then go down as collection from debtors is more than sales.

- ○ *Special Working Capital:* Special working capital is that rise in temporary working capital which occurs due to a special event which otherwise normally does not take place. It has no basis to forecast and has rare occurrence normally. For example, country where Olympic Games are held, all the business require extra working capital due to sudden rise in business activity.

It was all about the types of working capital. It needs to be managed with several working capital techniques so as to have the effective working capital management.

## Factors Determining Working Capital Requirement

Working capital requirement is influenced by various factors. In fact, any and every activity of a company affects the working capital requirements of the company. The magnitude of influence may be different. Some important of them are listed below:

## Factors Influencing Working Capital Management

**Nature of the Industry / Business:** The management of working capital is completely different from industry to industry. Simple comparison of service industry and manufacturing industry can clarify the point. In a service industry, there is no inventory and therefore one big component of working capital is already avoided. So, the nature of industry is a factor to determining the working capital requirement.

**Seasonality of Industry and Production Policy:** Businesses based on seasons like manufacturing of ACs whose demand peaks in summer and dips in winter. Requirement of working capital will be more in summer compared to winter if they are produced in the fashion of their demand. The policy of producing throughout the year can smoothen the fluctuation of working capital requirement.

**Competition:** If the industry is competitive, quick response to customer needs is compulsory and therefore higher level of inventory is maintained. Liberal credit terms are also mandatory with good service to survive in the market. So, higher the competition, higher would be the requirement of working capital.

**Production Cycle Time:** The production cycle time refers to the time required for converting the raw materials into finished goods. Higher this time, higher would be the time of blocking funds in the working capital.

**Credit Policy:** Liberal credit policy demands higher level of working capital and tight credit policy reduces it.

Growth and Expansion: Some industries are static and others are growing. Obviously, growing industry grows the requirement of working capital also as compared to static industry.

Raw Material Short Supply: If the raw material supply is not smooth for any reason, companies tend to store more of raw materials than needed and that increased requirement of working capital.

Net Cash Profit: Profit or retained earnings are one of the sources of working capital for the business. It will depend upon net cash profits as to how muchworking capital financing is required from external sources.

Taxes: Taxes are often paid in advance. This also blocks a part of working capital. Depending on the tax environment of the industry, working capital needs are also affected.

Dividend Policy: Dividend policy determines the level of retained profits with the business and retained profits are also used for working capital. This is how; dividend policy affects the need for working capital.

Price Levels: The price levels of inventory and other expenses such as labour rates etc increase the working capital requirement. If the company also is able to increase the price of their finished goods, it reduces this impact.

Other factors that determine or impact the working capital in some or the other way are as follows:

• Cash Requirements

• Volume of Sales

• Terms of Purchase and Sales

• Inventory Turnover

• Business Turnover

• Current Assets Requirements

• Profit Planning and Control

• Repayment Ability

• Cash Reserves

• Operation Efficiency

• Change in Technology

• Firm's Finance and Dividend Policy

• Attitude towards Risk

## *Principles of Working Capital Management*

Principles of Working Capital Management

The following are the principles of working capital management:

Principles of the risk variation— Risk here refers to the inability of firm to maintain sufficient current assets to pay its obligations. If working capital is varied relative to sales, the amount of risk that a firm assumes is also varied and the opportunity for gain or loss is increased. In other words, there is a definite relationship between the degree of risk and the rate of return. As a firm assumes more risk, the opportunity for gain or loss increases. As the level of working capital relative to sales decreases, the degree of risk increases. When the degree of risk increases, the opportunity for gain and loss also increases. Thus, if the level of working capital goes up, amount of risk goes down, and vice-versa, the opportunity for gain is like-wise adversely affected. 18 Principle of equity position— According to this principle, the amount of working capital invested in each component should be adequately justified by a firm's equity position. Every rupee invested in the working capital should contribute to the net worth of the firm.

Principle of cost of capital— This principle emphasizes that different sources of finance have different cost of capital. It should be remembered that the cost of capital moves inversely with risk. Thus, additional risk capital results in decline in the cost of capital.

Principle of maturity of payment— A company should make every effort to relate maturity of payments to its flow of internally generated funds. There should be the least disparity between the maturities of a firm's short-term debt instruments and its flow of internally generated funds, because a greater risk is generated with greater disparity. A margin of safety should, however, be provided for any short-term debt payment.

## COMPONENTS OF WORKING CAPITAL :

**Cash.** Cash is one of the most liquid and important components of working capital. Holding cash involves cost because the worth of cash held, after a year will be less than the value of cash as on today. Excess of cash balance should not be kept in business because cash is a non-earning asset.-Hence, a proper and judicious cash management is of utmost importance in business.

**Creditors :** It makes sense to pay your suppliers (your creditors) as and when their invoices become due but not before. Some franchisees pay their suppliers as soon as the cash becomes available. This is not a good use of your funds — the funds could be better used by being invested and earning interest or, possibly, buying more stock.

You should, however, try to pay your suppliers on their agreed terms. You expect your customers (your debtors) to pay you within your credit terms so you should try to do the same with your suppliers.

Rowarth points out how recent weather conditions in Australia have impacted franchisees in the building industry. After years of fine weather, heavy rains around the country have resulted in builders not being able to complete a stage and claim payment. Notwithstanding this, suppliers naturally require payment for work they have done. Rowarth says that "In these times it is particularly necessary for franchisees to micro manage their working capital — and it also emphasises the need for franchisees to have a good relationship with their bank manager."

If your suppliers offer you discounts for early settlement, then you should try to take advantage of those discounts. If, for example, a supplier offers a discount of 2.5 percent for paying on 30 day terms, and you take advantage of that discount each month, that is the equivalent of earning 30 percent on those funds over a year. It would be hard to find a better investment.

**Accounts Receivable.** Too many debtors always lock up the firm's resources especially during inflationary tendencies. This is a two step account. When goods are sold, inventories are reduced and accounts receivables are created. When payment is made, debtors reduce and cash level increases. Thus, quantum of debtors depends on two things, (i) volume of Credit sales (ii) average length of time between sales and collections. The entrepreneur should determine the optimal credit standards. An optimal credit policy should be established and the firm's operations should be continuously monitored to achieve higher sales and minimum bad debt losses.

**Inventory.** Inventories represent a substantial amount of firm's assets. Inventories must be properly managed so that this investment doesn't become too large, as it would result in blocked capital which could be put to productive use elsewhere. On the other hand, having too little or small inventory could result in loss of sales or loss of customer goodwill. An optimum level of inventory, therefore, should be maintained.

## OF MANAGEMENT OF WORKING CAPITAL

Monitoring of working capital management requires following procedure:- 2.8.1 Monitoring of components of working capital: Concerned manager should know as to how much funds have been blocked in cash, receivables, inventory, loan and advances on daily or weekly basis. He should also see whether funds blocked in components of the working capital are at optimal level, are as per firm's standard and as per industry norms. If there is any deviation, the reasons of the same should be analyzed for taking corrective measures. 2.8.2 Calculating the percentage of funds invested in working capital: In most of the companies huge funds are invested in working capital. Manager should make equilibrium between funds invested in fixed assets and working capital .He should know the affiliation between current and fixed assets and any deviation in the percentages of these funds may be analyzed accordingly for taking corrective measures. 2.8.3 Recording time spent in managing of working capital: In most companies substantial time is spent by the financial manager in managing of working capital. He should know as to how much time is being devoted by the members of finance department in managing working capital. This type of monitoring will assist him to propose an insight into the effective management of working capital. 2.9 STUDY OF MANAGEMENT OF WORKING CAPITAL Study of working capital management occupies a very prominent position in fiscal administration. It has not been acknowledged as so a good deal as in recent years. Working 36 capital management is an essential ingredient of overall fiscal administration. The field of working capital throws a welcome challenge and prospect to a financial manager. Working capital management has been looked at as the energetic place of a financial manager. The management of working capital is identical to the management of short period monetary liquidity. The magnitude of short time liquidity can most excellently be measured by investigating the repercussions which move from a lack of capability to shortterm liabilities. Inadequacy of liquidity implies lack of self-sufficiency of alternatives in addition to restrain management's liberty of progress. If deficiency of liquidity continues to be in trouble, it may eventually result in bankruptcy and economic failure. Thus, working capital management is associated with the sustained survival of a company, not withstanding production of quality goods, effectual selling, proficient manufacturing, and shrewd permanent resources management. Many organizations have lost the control of ownership since liquidity problem causes them to be captured by creditors, enforced amalgamation or insolvency. An admirable long run viewpoint for a company becomes irrelevant if control disappears in the short run. Working capital practices influence marketing, human resources, manufacturing and all that happens in the company is interrelated to working capital decisions. Working capital management, as an area, is connected with carrying out working capital functions. In each company, the working capital task ought to subsist in some form or the other. A study of working capital management is extremely significant for inside and outside professionals. Sales growth, dividend announcement, plant's extension, adding fresh merchandise line, enhancing of remuneration and increasing price level, et cetera, place additional burden on working capital management. Breakdown of every company is unquestionably due to pitiable management and nonexistence of managing proficiency. 37 Significance of management of working capital is due to considerable segment of whole investments which is positioned in current assets and altitude of current assets and current liabilities will alter rapidly with the deviation in sales. Nevertheless fixed assets outlay and long-term borrowing too will retort to the changes in sales, however its retort will be feeble. 2.10 CONCEPTUAL FRAMEWORK OF WORKING CAPITAL In order to understand conceptual framework of management of working capital it is necessary to go through principle of working capital, accounts receivable management, inventory management, cash management, payable management and financing of working capital. 2.10.1 Working capital-meaning and definitions Money is required equally for purchasing fixed assets as well as for operating functions of a company. For operating day-to-day business activities money is used for procuring raw materials, processing these into completed goods and finally handing over the same to the customers. The finance for meeting such working expenditure is frequently referred to as 'working capital'. Working capital also refers to the circulating capital essential to meet the routine operations of a company. Working capital defined by some of authors is as follow:- 1. "Working capital refers to a firm's investment in short term assets such as cash amounts receivables, inventories etc".-- Weston & Brigham 2. "Working capital means current assets"--Mead, Baker and Malott 3. "The sum of the current assets is the working capital of the business". -- J.S. Mill 4. "Working capital is the amount of funds necessary to cover the cost of operating the enterprise. Working capital in a going concern is a revolving fund; it consists of cash receipts from sales which are used to cover the cost of current operations"-- 38 Johan A. Shubin 5. "Working capital is made up of combination of several current assets, such as cash, inventory, and accounts receivable, and is used to identify a business's liquidity condition"--Steve Martin. 6. "Working capital, in simple term, is the amount of funds which a company must have to finance its day to day operations. It can be regarded as that proportion of company's total capital which is employed in short term operations"— V.E.Ramamoorthy. Working capital is surplus of the current assets in excess of current liabilities and provisions. However as stated in accounting terminology, it is variation between the inflow and outflow of money. Working capital includes stocks of material, fuels, work in progress, completed commodities, by-products, cash in hand, bank balance, loan & advance and receivables. The term "working capital" is frequently referred to "circulating capital" which is often used to indicate those possessions which are altered with relative velocity from one form to another i.e. beginning from cash, altering to raw materials, converting into work in progress and completed goods, sale of finished goods and finally back to cash with receipt of cash from debtors. Working capital has been described as the "life blood" of any business which is appropriate since it constitutes a clockwork-like flowing watercourse throughout the business. 2.10.2 Working capital-Concept There are two concepts of working capital, that is to say gross concept and net concept, which are elaborated as under:- Gross working capital: According to this concept, gross working capital refers to the company's outlay in current assets. Current assets are those assets which can be transformed into cash during an accounting period and comprise cash, short-term 39 securities, receivable, loan & advance and inventory. The sum of current liabilities is not subtracted from the total of current assets. This concept views Working Capital and total of Current Assets as two identical terms. This concept is also treated as `Current Capital' otherwise `Circulating Capital'. One additional facet of the gross working capital points to the call for arranging finances to funding current assets. Whenever a requirement for working capital funds occurs owing to the escalating intensity of company operation or for any supplementary reason, funding arrangement ought to be made immediately. Similarly, if suddenly, some spare sources occur these should not be permitted to stay idle, but must be invested in temporary securities. Thus the financial executive is supposed to have information about the origin and sources, of working capital funds as well as alternative outlay where redundant sources may be for the time being, are invested. Net working capital: According to this concept, net working capital refers to the difference between current assets and current liabilities. Current liabilities are those claims of outsiders, which are likely to be paid within a financial year and usually comprise creditors, bills payable, bank loans and outstanding expenditure. Net working capital may be positive or negative. When current liabilities are in excess of current assets, then negative working capital arises. Net working capital is a qualitative concept. It shows the liquidity situation of the company and presages the level to which working capital requirements will possibly be financed by fixed sources of funds. Current assets supposed to be adequately in surplus of current liabilities to provide an edge or buffer for meeting obligations within the normal operating cycle of a company's operation. Sequentially to defend their interests, short-term creditors always like a company to preserve current assets at an upper level than current liabilities. However the eminence of current assets ought to be well thought-out in deciding the stage of current liabilities. However, the superiority of 40 current assets ought to be measured in deciding the level of current assets vis-a-vis current liabilities. Poor liquidity situation poses a danger to the solvency of the company and makes it insecure. A negative working capital leads to negative liquidity, and possibly will confirm to be dangerous for the company's goodwill. Too much liquidity is also not good. It possibly will be owing to negligence in management of current assets. Therefore, without delay and appropriate action ought to be taken by administration to get better and correct the imbalances in the liquidity position of a company. Net working capital concept also covers the query of well judged blend of long-term and short-term sources for funding current assets. For each company, there is a small amount of net working capital which is fixed. Therefore, a segment of the working capital ought to be funded with the equity share capital, debentures, long-term loans, preference share capital or plough back of profits. Administration may, therefore, take a decision to the extent by which current assets ought to be funded with equity capital and/or on loan capital. The two concepts of working capital-gross and net are not exclusive; relatively these have equivalent importance from the administration viewpoint. The gross working capital concept concentrates notice on aspects of current assets management as to how to optimize outlay in current assets and how to finance the current assets. The contemplation of the altitude of outlay in current assets should be just at optimal level, not more nor less, to the requirements of the company. Too much outlay in current assets ought to be avoided since it impairs the company's viability, as inoperative outlay produces nothing. Alternatively, insufficient amount of working capital can intimidate solvency of the company since its incapability to pay its current liabilities. It ought to be sensed that the working capital requirements of the company may be changeable with varying operational activities. It possibly will cause surplus or scarcity of working capital recurrently. The administration 41 should be quick to kick off an action and set the imbalances right. In a nutshell it may be pertinent, to note that both gross and net concepts of working capital are evenly significant for the resourceful administration of working capital. There is no short cut way to decide the accurate quantity of gross or net working capital for any company. The data and problems of every company ought to be analyzed to decide the quantity of working capital. There is no precise regulation as to how current assets ought to be funded. It is not viable to put into practice, the financing of current assets by short-term funds only. Keeping in mind the parameters of the company, a well judged blend of long and short-term funds ought to be invested in current assets. In view of reality, those current assets occupy cost of funds; these ought to be put to creative use. 2.10.3 Kinds of working capital Generally, working capital is of two types; fixed working capital and fluctuating working capital. Both these types of working capital; permanent and temporary-are needed to make possible production and sales by the operating cycle, but temporary working capital is maintained by the company to fulfill the liquidity necessities that are expected to be temporary. Fixed working capital: The necessity for current assets is connected with the operating cycle, which is an uninterrupted course of action. As such, the requirement for current assets is felt continuously. The amount of investment in current assets on the other hand may not all the time be the same. The requirement for investment in current assets may possibly go up or down over a period of time according to the altitude of production. However, there is a definite minimum level of current assets all the time, which is necessary for the company to maintain in its business irrespective of the level of business activities. This is the fixed minimum level necessary for keeping the flow of the current 42 assets. This minimum level of investment in current assets is everlastingly blocked up in business and is for that reason called as permanent or fixed or regular working capital. It is fixed in the same way as investment in the company's fixed assets is. Fluctuating working capital: Requirement for working capital, over and above the fixed working capital, will rise and fall in relation to variations in production and sales of the company. The requirement for working capital may also differ on account of cyclic variations, irregular and unexpected situations. An increase in the price possibly will lead to an increase in the volume of funds invested in stock of raw materials in addition to finished products. Extra quantum of working capital may possibly be needed to face aggressive contest in the market or other emergencies like strikes and lockouts. Any extraordinary publicity campaigns arranged for increasing sales or other promotional operations may have to be funded by extra working capital. The additional working capital required to face the fluctuating business activities is called the fluctuating or variable working capital. 2.11 NEED OF WORKING CAPITAL The requirement of working capital to operate the day-to-day activities relating to the business of the company hardly needs to be overemphasized. We will barely come across a company which does not have need of any sum of working capital. Definitely companies vary in their necessities of the working capital. We are familiar with the fact that a company should endeavor to maximize the possessions of its stakeholders. In its attempt to do so, a company ought to produce adequate return from its business. Earning a stable amount of income requires flourishing sales activities. The company has to put enough funds in current assets for creating sales. Current assets are required since sales do not translate into cash immediately. There is an eternal operating cycle caught up in the 43 process of the alteration of sales into cash. There is dissimilarity between current and fixed assets in expressions of their liquidity. A company requires a lot of years to recuperate the preliminary outlay in fixed assets such as plant and machinery or land and building. On the other hand, outlay in current assets is turned over several times in a year. Outlay in current assets such as inventories and accounts receivable is realized during the company's operating cycle which is typically less than a year. Operating cycle is the time period requisite to convert raw material into finished goods, finished goods to sale and sale to cash. The operating cycle concept is not only linked to manufacturing companies. Nonmanufacturing companies such as wholesalers and retailers will not comprise the manufacturing stage. They will obtain inventory of finished products and change them into receivables and receivables into cash. Further, service and financial sector companies will not have stocks of goods. Their inventory will be cash. Their operating cycles will be the shortest. They require obtaining cash, then lending to the debtors and again converting lending back into cash. The requirement of current assets emerges due to operating cycle. The operating cycle is an uninterrupted course of action and, therefore, the requirement of current assets is felt continuously. However the degree of current assets required is not the same for all time, it goes upward and downward during the operation. However, there is forever a small amount of current assets which are always needed by the company to carry on its business activities. This smallest level of current assets is referred to as fixed working capital. It is fixed in the same way as the company's permanent assets are. Depending on the changes in manufacturing and sales, the requirement for working capital, over and above the fixed working capital, will fluctuate. The additional working capital, required to carry the varying manufacturing and sales 44 operations is called fluctuating, or variable, or provisional working capital. Both types of working capitals-permanent and provisional-are essential to make possible manufacturing and sale through the operating cycle, but provisional-working capital is formed by the company to meet liquidity necessities that will last only temporarily. 2.12 OPTIMAL LEVEL OF WORKING CAPITAL The company ought to keep a sound working capital position. It should have sufficient working capital to operate its business activities. Both redundant as well as insufficient working capital positions are hazardous from the company's viewpoint. Redundant working capital means inactive funds which produce no gains for the company. Scarcity of working capital not only impairs the company's productivity but also leads furthermore to manufacturing hindrances and inefficiencies. 2.12.1 Advantage of maintaining working capital at optimal level Some of the major advantages of keeping working capital at optimal level are as under:- Solvency of the company: Satisfactory working capital helps in keeping solvency of the company by supplying continuous flow of production. Reputation: Adequate working capital enables a company to disburse timely payments and therefore, helps in creating and keeping reputation. Unproblematic Loans: A company having sufficient working capital, high solvency and excellent credit position is able to get loans from banks and other sources on friendly and constructive terms. Cash discounts: Adequate working capital furthermore enables a company to get benefit of cash discounts on the procurements and therefore, it reduces costs. Uninterrupted delivery of raw material: Adequate working capital assures uninterrupted receipt of raw material for the nonstop production. Uninterrupted disbursement of salaries wages and other day-to-day obligations: A 45 company which has sufficient working capital will be able to make usual disbursement of salaries, wages and other day-to-day obligations which raise the spirits of its employees, increase their effectiveness, decrease wastages, save costs and increase profits. Utilization of positive market conditions: Simply a company which has sufficient working capital can utilize positive market situation such as procuring its necessities of material in bulk when the prices are low and by holding its inventory for privileged prices. Capability to face crisis: Sufficient working capital makes a company able to face business crisis in emergencies such as depression for the reason that during such periods, generally, there is much burden on working capital. Rapid and interrupted return on investment: Every saver desires a rapid and interrupted return on his savings. Adequacy of working capital makes a company able to disburse dividends rapidly to its investors as there possibly will not be much force to plough back earnings. This increases the self-confidence of its investors and creates an encouraging market to acquire further funds. Sky-scraping morale: Sufficiency of working capital makes an atmosphere of safety, confidence, high morale and creates effectiveness in a company, on the whole. 2.12.3 Redundant or insufficient working capital Every company ought to have sufficient working capital to operate its business activities. It ought to contain neither redundant nor insufficient working capital. Redundant as well as inadequate working capital positions are awful for any company. However, out of the two, it is the insufficiency of working capital, which is more hazardous from the point of view of the company. Disadvantages of redundant working capital Redundant working capital means idle sources which make no earnings for the company and therefore the company cannot make an appropriate profit on its investments. 46 o When there is an excessive working capital it possibly will lead to the needless procurement and buildup of inventory attracting more probability of burglary, waste and losses. o Redundant working capital implies too much debtors and faulty credit practices which may create elevated occurrence of bad debts. o It may lead to incompetency of the company, on the whole. o Owing to less rate of return on funds the worth of shares may as well decrease. o The excessive working capital may raise speculative transactions. Disadvantages or dangers of insufficient working capital o A company which has insufficient working capital will not be able to meet its short-term obligations in time. Therefore, it will lose its goodwill and shall not be capable of getting superior credit facilities. o It cannot procure its necessities in bulk and cannot avail discounts. o It becomes difficult for the company to take advantage of positive market situation and take on lucrative projects owing to lack of working capital. o The company will not be able to disburse day-to-day expenditure of its business activities and this may lead to inefficiencies and inflated expenses and finally decrease the earning of the company. o It becomes infeasible to exploit competently the fixed assets owing to non availability of liquid sources. 2.13 Determinants of working capital Indian Industries nowadays have worth maximization as the main purpose and to attain it one ought to be competent of anticipating the necessities of working capital correctly. Both unnecessary and insufficient investments in working capital components are dangerous for a company. Therefore, the finance executive has to scrutinize all the factors which decide 47 the working capital necessities within the hypothetical and realistic points of view. The hypothetical considerations from time to time control the tactic of assessment; whilst the company is forced to follow the restrictions forced by the borrowers. The finance executive, therefore, ought to think all the factors that have a bearing on the working capital as well as on the cash, receivables and inventory. There are no laid down regulations or formulae to decide the working capital necessity of a company. A huge number of factors, every one having a diverse significance, affect the working capital requirement of a company. Also, the magnitude of factors varies for a company over time. Therefore, a study of applicable factors ought to be made in turn to settle on total investment in working capital. It is not probable to grade determinants of working capital since all such factors are of various degrees of significance and the power of individual factor may vary for a company over time. The following are vital factors normally affecting the working capital necessities of a company: - Environment of Businessϖ Sales and Demand Conditionsϖ Technology and production policyϖ Credit Policyϖ Availability of Creditϖ Working effectivenessϖ Changes in price levelϖ

## 2.14 ESTIMATING WORKING CAPITAL REQUIREMENTS

As working capital is treated as livelihood and controlling nerve centre of operational activities of a company, no business lacking a sufficient quantity of working capital can be run effectively. To avoid the scarcity of working capital continuously, an approximation of working capital needs ought to be prepared beforehand so that preparations can be made to acquire ample working capital. Main befitting technique of estimating the working capital requirements of a business concern is the theory of operating cycle. On the other hand, various other techniques in practice can be applied to decide working capital needs. Under mentioned, are some of techniques which are currently being applied effectively:- • Ratio of sales technique • Regression analysis technique • Cash forecasting technique • Operating cycle technique • Projected balance sheet technique

## 2.15 MANAGEMENT OF COMPONENTS OF WORKING CAPITAL

2.15.1 Management of inventory Most important part of working capital is inventory in majority of companies of India. On an average, inventories are roughly sixty per cent of working capital in Indian companies. For the reason that large volume of inventories are kept by companies, a substantial sum of funds is necessary to be devoted to them. It is, consequently, extremely important to administer inventories efficiently and effectively in order to keep away from needless investment. A company ignoring the management of inventories will be jeopardizing its 49 long-run productivity and may fall short ultimately. It is likely for a company to decrease its levels of inventories to a substantial degree, without any unfavorable impact on production and sales, by using simple inventory planning and control techniques. The reduction in 'too much' inventories carries a favorable effect on profitability of company.

Components of inventory Inventories are stock of the goods a company is producing for sale and various ingredients which make up that product. The different forms in which inventories subsist in a manufacturing company are:- o Raw materials o Work-in-process o Finished goods o Stores and spares Need for inventory Some quantity of inventory on one hand is required for day-to-day operations of a company, and on the other hand, keeping unwarranted inventory will obstruct the sources and cost more to the company. There are many other related costs of keeping unwarranted inventory. Managers should estimate the level of inventory for day-to-day operation of the company's activities. Following are some of the prime reasons for keeping inventories which are applicable to various ingredients of inventory: Objectives of inventory management Major objectives of inventory management are: a) to keep inventory at optimal level for well-organized and smooth operation of production and sales. b) To invest smallest amount in inventories to maximize profitability. Unnecessary and insufficient inventories are not advantageous. These are two risky levels 50 within which the company ought to function. The purpose of inventory management ought to be decided and kept at most favorable level of inventory outlay. The optimum level of inventory will lie between the two risky points of redundant and insufficient inventory. The company must forever keep away from a situation of over- investment or underinvestment in inventory. The foremost danger of over investment is needless hold-up of the company's sources and loss of earnings. Second danger of redundant inventory is burden of carrying costs, and risk of liquidity. The unnecessary level of inventory consumes sources of the company, which cannot be used for any other purpose, and therefore, it contains an opportunity cost. Inventory carrying expenses, such as the expenses of storage space, handling, insurance and check up, also increase in percentage to the quantity of inventory. These expenses will weaken the company's productivity. Too much inventory carried for long-period increase probability of failure of liquidity. It may not be likely to sell products in due course and at full worth. Raw materials are usually more difficult to sell as compared to finish products even as the holding time increases. There are extraordinary situations when it possibly will cost the company dearly for holding stocks of raw materials. This is possible under situation of price increase and shortage. Work-inprogress is far more complicated to sell. Likewise, problems may be faced to sell off completed products inventory as period extends. The descending shifts in market and the cyclic factors may result in selling finished products at low rates. One other risk of keeping too much inventory is the physical corrosion of inventory whilst in warehouse. Keeping an insufficient level of inventory is quite risky. The foremost risk of underinvestment in inventory includes production hold-ups and breakdown to meet supply commitments. Insufficient raw materials and work-in-progress inventory will result in recurrent manufacturing interruptions.

Likewise, if completed product inventory is not adequate to meet the requirements of purchasers smoothly, they possibly will move to the 51 products of competitors, which will amount to an everlasting loss to the company. The objective of inventory management, therefore, ought to be to kept away from unnecessary and insufficient levels of inventory and to keep adequate inventory for the smooth manufacturing and sales activities. Efforts ought to be carried out to give a requisition at the proper time with the accurate source to procure the correct size at genuine rates and quality.

## 2.15.2 MANAGEMENT OF RECEIVABLES

Tendency of taking goods and services on credit is progressively gaining significance in the way of livelihood of the Indians. Alternatively, customer credit has turned out to be the main selling factor. When customers wait for credit, trade units in turn wait for credit from their vendors to go with their investment in credit extended to customers. An effective administrative control requires suitable administration of liquid assets and inventory. These assets are an ingredient of working capital of the company. A well-organized utilization of fiscal sources is essential to keep away from financial problems. Receivables take place when a company sells its goods or services on credit and does not get cash immediately. It is an indispensable marketing instrument, performing as a link for the movement of products in the course of manufacturing and delivery stages to consumers. A company allows trade credit to defend its sales from the competitors and to be a focus for the possible customers to purchase its goods at favorable conditions. Trade credit creates receivable which the company is estimated to accumulate in the near future. The receivable arising out of credit has three unique features; first, it contains an aspect of risk which ought to be vigilantly analyzed. Second, it is based on monetary worth to the purchaser, the economic value in goods or services passes instantly on the occasion of sale, whilst the seller expects an equal worth to be received afterwards. Third, it implies futurity. 52 The cash disbursement for products or services received by the purchaser will be made by him in an upcoming period. The customers from whom receivable or book debts have to be collected in the future are called trade debtors or plainly as debtors and stand for the company's claim on asset. Receivables occupy a considerable segment of current assets of several companies. In India, receivables, after inventories, comprise the main ingredient of current assets. They constitute about one-third of current assets. Allowing credit and creating receivables tantamount to the blocking of the company's sources. The gap between the date of sale and the date of receipt of payment has to be financed out of working capital. This necessitates the company to get funds from banks or other sources. Therefore, receivables represent investment. As considerable amounts are blocked-up in receivables, it requires vigilant investigation and appropriate management. Factoring of receivables Receivable management is a focused activity, and requires a lot of time and hard work from financial executives of the company. Realization of receivables creates a trouble, mainly for small companies. Banks have the strategy of funding receivables. On the other hand, this help is obtainable for a limited time and the sellers of products and services have to tolerate the danger of non-payment by debtors. Work relating to receivable management may be assigned to a specialist of an organization for efficient and effective realization of receivables. This type of activity is called factoring. Factoring is a well-known method of administrating, funding and realizing receivables. In India some banks and financial institutes and their subsidiaries use it to make available factoring services to their clients.

### 2.15.3 MANAGEMENT OF CASH

Cash is essential input to establish a business unit. Initially cash is invested in fixed assets like plant and machinery, which facilitates the company to manufacture products and 53 produce cash by selling them. Cash is the significant component of working capital for the operational activities of a company. Cash is the indispensable input required to keep the business going on an uninterrupted basis; it is also eventual output anticipated to be realized by selling the service or goods produced by the company. The company ought to maintain adequate cash, neither extra nor inadequate. Cash scarcity will disturb the company's production activities whereas unnecessary cash will merely stay idle, with no contribution towards the profitability of the company. Therefore, the main task of the financial manager is to keep sound cash position. Cash is the currency which a company can pay out instantly with no constraint.

The word cash includes coins, currency and cheques in custody of the company, and balances in its bank accounts. Sometimes near-cash items, such as marketable securities or time deposits of the banks, are also incorporated in cash. The essential feature of near-cash property is that these can willingly be transformed into cash. Normally, when a company has surplus cash, it invests it in marketable securities. This type of outlay contributes some profit to the company. In the framework of working capital management, cash management refers to optimizing the benefits and expenditure linked with keeping cash. As described previously, if the cash is not put into use, there is no advantage derived out just by maintaining it. Further, keeping cash with no purpose as well costs the company either directly in the shape of interest or opportunity profits that could be earned out of the cash.

At the same time, it is not possible to operate the company without keeping cash. Aspects of management of cash Management of cash is related to the managing of inflow and outflow of cash, cash balances kept by the company, financing deficit or investing surplus cash. Cash is generated by sales and disbursed for purchases and other expenses. Management of cash 54 requires to complete this cycle at the lowest and to maintain adequate liquidity. Cash management assumes extra significance than other components of working capital since cash is the most important but the least industrious component of working capital. It is important since it is utilized to disburse the company's commitments. On the other hand, cash is infertile.

Contrasting fixed assets or inventory, it does not manufacture products for sale. For that reason, the endeavor of management of cash is to keep ample control over cash position to maintain the adequate liquidity and to utilize surplus cash in a number of lucrative opportunities. Cash management is also significant since it is not easy to forecast cash flows, exactly, mainly the inflows, and there is no coincidence amid the receipt and disbursement of cash.

Cash management is equally essential because cash constitutes the nominal segment of the whole current assets; however management's substantial time is required to manage it. During some periods, cash outflows will exceed cash inflows, because payments for taxes, dividends, or seasonal inventory build up. At other times, cash inflow will be more than cash payments because there may be large cash sales and debtors may be realized in large sums promptly. In the recent past, a large number of innovations have been undertaken in cash management techniques. An obvious aim of the firm now-a-days is to manage its cash affairs in such a way as to keep cash balance at a minimum level and to invest the surplus cash in profitable investment opportunities. Objectives of keeping cash

Investment in cash is the least industrious asset. Over and over again, company is not reliant on this asset in the production procedure nor is necessary for creating inventory or selling. Therefore, the essential query is as to why companies keep cash. 55 Management of surplus cash Profit making companies have to generate extra cash at the end of operating cycle because the cash received from debtors is larger than cash invested at the start. Though, actually, many profit making companies observe impact of negative flow of cash. There are numerous reasons for this position. The disparity between inflows and outflows and transfer of short-term funds for long-term requirements are two main reasons for this situation. Although it is not advantageous to use the short term funds for long-term requirements, often companies choose their route to transfer if there is some delay in getting funds from long-term sources. The position is set right once the company receives the long-term funds. In other words, profit-making companies occasionally create spare cash even though they face heaviness on cash flows in other times. The question is how to deal with such spare cash. Surplus cash balance is the least creative asset of the company and therefore, should be minimized. Cash needs that are obtained from defensive or speculative motives can typically be fulfilled in the shape of liquid financial investments, that is, savings that can be easily transformed into cash. Though, many companies experience cyclic cash needs, which may end result from cyclic payments and/or collections those are not coordinated with each other, finance managers are often anxious about finding well-organized ways of stocking surplus cash. That's why, there are positions in which company finds it optimal to invest part of their cash balances in the shape of marketable securities, which give a certain profit and can be transformed into cash at very little notice. As the reasons for these investments are strongly related to the purpose for maintaining liquidity, those investments which satisfy the parameters of protection and liquidity, should be well thought-out.

## 2.15.4 MANAGEMENT OF PAYABLES

Purchases of goods and services create a commercial credit for both the sellers and the buyers. Account payables generally stand for a huge segment of company's liabilities. A considerable segment of procurement of products and services in a company are on more credit conditions to a certain extent than against cash payment. Whereas the seller of products and services is likely to recognize credit as a force for increasing sales or as a shape of non-price tool of competition, the purchaser is likely to look upon it as a loaning of products or inventory. The seller's credit is called as Accounts Payable, Trade Credit, Trade Bill, Trade Acceptance, Commercial Draft or Bills Payable depending on the character of credit granted. Trade credits or payables comprise the main part of current liabilities in a lot of business companies. And they are mainly funding the inventory which forms the most important chunk of current assets in a lot of companies. Stretching of payables It is usually understood that the payment to the seller is disbursed within due time. On the other hand, a company may put off payment ahead of due date. This kind of deferment is called stretching on the trade. The cost of stretching accounts payable is two-fold: the cost due to loss of cash discount and the likely worsening in the credit ranking. If a company stretches its payables exceptionally, so that its payables are considerably offending, its credit rating will suffer. Seller will analyze the company with uneasiness and may be firm or quite stern on conditions of sale. Even though it is not easy to calculate, there is definitely an opportunity cost to a worsening in the company's quality of payment. Effectual management of payables Significant points to be kept in mind for effectual management of payables are as under:- Bargain and get the most positive credit conditions consistent with the existing business practice relating to the concerned merchandise line.

Where cash discount is obtainable for timely payments, take benefit of the offer and obtain the savings from that. Where cash discount is not obtainable, clear up the payable on its due date and not in advance. It pays benefit of full credit time. Do not extend payables outside the due date, except in unavoidable circumstances, as such delays in meeting obligations have unfavorable effects on purchaser's trustworthiness and may affect more rigorous credit conditions, refutation of credit or high prices on products and services purchased. Maintain strong financial position and a good follow up of past record of transactions with the seller so that it would maintain his self-belief. The quantum and the conditions of credit are mostly impacted by seller's appraisal of buyer's fiscal wellbeing and capability to meet maturing commitments quickly. During extreme aggressive position, seller may be eager to extend credit restrictions and times. Evaluate your power to negotiate and get the most excellent potential transaction. Avoid tendency relating to diverting payables. Keep the self liquidating nature of payables and do not utilize the means acquired there from for purchasing fixed assets. Payables are intended to flow through current assets and quickly get transformed into cash from sales for meeting those short term commitments which are likely to mature in the near future. Maintain a regular check on cases of negligence. Delays in finalization of payables within the stipulated time can be classified into age groups to spot delays by more than one month, two months, three months, etc. Once overdue payables are given main concern of concentration for payment, the negligence rate can be decreased or eliminated totally.

## 2.16 FINANCING OF WORKING CAPITAL

2.16.1 Practices of financing of working capital A company generally applies following type of practices for financing of working capital:- Long-term financing: The resource of long-term funding comprises ordinary share capital, preference share capital, debentures, long-term loans from financial institutions/ banks and retained earnings. Short-term financing: The short-term funding is taken for a time less than one year. It is taken in advance from banks and other lenders of short-term funding in the money market. Short-term funding comprises working capital loan from banks, public deposits, commercial papers, factoring of accounts receivables, etc. Spontaneous financing: Spontaneous financing refers to the unplanned sources of shortterm funding arising in the ordinary course of a business. Trade supplier's credit and outstanding expenditures are examples of spontaneous funding. There is no clear cost of spontaneous funding. A company is likely to make use of these sources of funding to the fullest level. The actual option of funding current assets, once the spontaneous means of funding have been entirely used, is between the long-term and short-term sources of funding.

2.16.2 Practices generally followed by companies to finance working capital Conservative approach: A company in practice may apply a conservative approach in funding its current and fixed assets. The funding practices of the business is said to be conservative when it relies more on long-term sources for working capital needs. Under a conservative arrangement, the company funds its permanent assets and as well part of temporary current assets with long-term funds. In the periods when the company has no requirement for temporary currents assets, the redundant long-term funds can be utilized in 59 the marketable securities to preserve liquidity. The conservative practices depend a lot on long-term funds and, consequently, the company has less menace of facing the difficulty of deficiency of resources. Aggressive approach: A company could be aggressive in funding its assets, when it is said to be followed by the company utilizing more short-term funds than required by the matching program. Under an aggressive strategy, the company funds a fraction of its permanent current assets with short-term sources. Some exceptionally aggressive companies may still finance a fraction of their fixed assets with short-term funds. More utilization of short-term funds makes the company more unsafe. Matching approach: A company can apply a financial plan which matches the predictable life of assets with the projected life of the means of funds raised for funding assets. Thus, a long-term loan may be raised to fund a fixed asset with an anticipated life of more than one year; on the other hand current asset to be sold during a short period may be funded with a short-term source like commercial paper or a bank borrowing. The good reason for the exact matching is that, because the rationale of funding is to pay for assets, the method of funding and the asset should be relinquished at the same time. Utilizing long-term assets with short-term funding is expensive in addition to problematic as arrangement for the new short-term funding will have to be made on a routine basis. When a company adopts matching approach popularly known as hedging approach, long- term funds will be utilized to finance fixed assets and permanent current assets, short-term funds for funding provisional or changeable current assets. Though, it should be kept in mind that accurate matching is not feasible due to uncertainty regarding the projected life of assets.

2.16.3 Type of short-term financing Funds which are presented for a period of one year or less than one year are called short-range finance. Short-term finances are utilized for funding of working capital. Most important short- 60 range means of funds for working capital are: business credit and bank loans. The utilization of business credit has been going upward over years in India. Bank loan is the subsequent significant means of working capital financing. Following are the main constituents of the short term financing:- Trade credit Business credit is that credit which a purchaser gets from seller of products in the usual course of business. Practically, the purchasing company does not have to disburse payment instantly for the procurement made. This deferment of payments is a short-term funding which is called trade credit. It is the most important means of funding working capital of company. Small companies are greatly reliant on business credit as a means of funding of working capital, because they find it complicated to have funds from other sources. Business credit is typically a casual arrangement, and is arranged on an open account basis. A seller supplies products to the purchaser on credit which the buyer accepts, and therefore, in effect, agrees to pay the amount due as per sales condition in the bill. On the other hand, he does not officially concede it as a debt; he does not sign any official instrument. Once the trade links have been recognized between the buyer and the seller, they have each other's mutual assurance, and business credit becomes a regular action which may be occasionally reviewed by the supplier. Open account trade credit appears as sundry creditors on the buyer's balance sheet. Business credit may also take the shape of bills payable. When the buyer signs a bill to obtain credit on trade, it appears on as bills payable on the buyer's balance sheet. The bill has a particular upcoming date, and is regularly used when the seller is less confident about the buyer's eagerness and capability to pay, or when the seller needs cash by discounting the bill for a bank. A bill is prescribed acknowledgement of a commitment to pay back the outstanding amount. Accrued Expenses Accrued expenses denote a liability that a company has to disburse for the service which it has previously received. Thus they denote spontaneous, without interest means of funding. The most significant constituent of accruals are wages and salaries, taxes and interest. Accrued wages and salaries denote obligations payable by the company to its employees. Accrued taxes and interest form one more means of financing. This is a delayed payment of the company's commitment and therefore, is a mean of finance. It is a partial source of financing working capital. Deferred Income Deferred income denotes sources received by the company for products and services which it has contracted to supply in future. These proceeds increase the company's liquidity in the shape of cash; as a result, they comprise a significant means of financing. Payments which were made by customers in advance comprise the major constituents of deferred income. These payments are ordinary in case of costly goods, where the product is in short supply and the seller has a tough bargaining power as compared to the buyer. These payments are not recorded as income until products and services have been supplied to the purchaser. They are, therefore, shown as a liability in the company's balance sheet. Bank loans Banks are the most important source of financing working capital. After business credit, bank credit is the most significant means of financing working capital necessities of companies. A bank considers a company's sales and production strategy and the advantageous levels of current assets in deciding its working capital necessities. The sum sanctioned by the bank for the working capital of company is called credit limit. Credit limit is the highest amount of funds which a company can acquire from the bank. In the case of company with cyclic businesses, bank may fix separate limits for the 'peak level' credit necessities and 'normal non-peak level' credit necessities representing the time during which the separate limits will be used by the borrower. Practically, banks do not provide cent percent credit limit; they subtract some margin money. Margin constraints are based on the principle of conservatism and it is intended to make sure safety measures are taken by the banks before extending loans. Commercial papers Commercial paper is a different way of acquiring short term finances by well rated corporate borrowers for the purpose of working capital. A commercial paper at the same time gives a chance to cash rich investors to invest their funds in short term investments. It is a significant money market mechanism for acquiring short term sources. The Reserve Bank of India introduced commercial paper in the Indian money market on the suggestions of the Working Group on Money Market (Vaghul Committee). Only big companies having good credit ranking and sound fiscal position are capable of issue commercial paper to acquire short-term sources. The Reserve Bank of India has issued a number of guidelines to decide the eligibility of a company for the issue of commercial paper. Only a company which is listed on the stock exchange has prescribed net worth and maximum allowable bank funding can issue commercial paper up to the fixed percentage of its working capital limit. The maturity time of commercial paper, in India, generally ranges from 91 days to 180 days. It is sold at a concession from its face price and redeemed at face value on its due date. Hence, the cost of acquiring finances, through this source, is a role of the amount of concession and the time of due date and no interest rate is fixed by Reserve Bank of India for this purpose. Commercial paper is generally purchased by investors including banks, insurance companies, unit trusts and companies to invest spare funds for a short-time. A number of credit rating organizations like CRISIL, ICRA, CARE, DCR, SAMERA and 63 ONICRA etc; have been set up in India to rate commercial papers. Commercial paper is a less costly source of raising short-term funds as compared to the bank credit and proves to be effectual even at the time of rigid terms of bank credit. On the other hand, it can be utilized as a source of funding only by big companies having high credit rating and sound financial position. One more drawback of commercial paper is that it cannot be redeemed earlier than the due date even if the issuing company has spare funds for repayments.

## Disadvantages Of Insufficient Working Capital

The amount of working capital should be sufficient. Inadequate amount of working capital may create a lot of financial problems in business. Sometimes, inadequate working capital may be the major causes for closing down the business organization. Due to shortage of working capital, raw materials can not be purchased on time and payment of labor and other expenses can not be made on time. The disadvantages suffered by a firm with insufficient working capital are as follows:

1. The firm is unable to take advantages of new opportunities or adapt to change.

2. Trade discounts are lost. A firm with sufficient working capital is able to finance larger stocks and can therefore place large orders.

3. Cash discounts are lost. Some firms will try to persuade their debtors to pay early by offering cash discounts.

4. The advantages of being able to offer a credit line to customers are forgone.

5. Financial reputation is lost due to non-payment of trade creditors on time.

6. Creditors may apply to the court for winding up if the firm fails to pay their obligations on time.

# CHAPTER 4

# COST OF CAPITAL & CAPITAL BUDGETING

## *Introduction Of Cost Of Capital*

Investment decision is major decision for an organization. Under investment decision process, the cost and benefit of prospective projects is analyzed and the best alternative is selected on the basis of the result of analysis. The benchmark of computing present value and comparing the profitability of different investment alternatives is cost of capital. Cost of capital is also known as minimum required rate of return, weighted average cost of capital, cut off rate, hurdle rate, standard return etc. Cost of capital is determined on the basis of component cost of financing and proportion of these sources in capital structure.

## *Meaning Of Cost Of Capital*

Business firms raise the needed fund from internal sources and external sources. Undistributed and retained profit is the main source of internal fund. External fund is raised either by the issue of shares or by issue of debenture (debt) or by both means. The fund collected by any means is not cost free. Interest is to be paid on the fund obtained as debt and dividend is to be paid on the fund collected through the issue of shares. The average cost rate of different sources of fund is known as cost of capital. From the view point of return, cost of capital is the minimum required rate of return to be earned on investment.

In other words, the earning rate of a firm which is just sufficient to satisfy the expectation of the contributors of capital is called cost of capital. Shareholders and debenture holders are the contributors of the capital. For example, a firm needs 5,00,000 for investing in a new project. The firm can collect 3,00,000 from shares on which it must pay 12% dividend and 2,00,000 from debentures on which it must pay 7% interest. If the fund is raised and invested in the project, the firm must earn at least 50,000 which becomes sufficient to pay 36,000 dividend(12% of 3,00,000) and 14000 interest(7% of 2,00,000). The required earning 50,000 is 12% of the total fund raised. This 12% rate of return is called cost of capital.

In this way, cost of capital is only minimum required rate of return to earn on investment and it is not the actual earning rate of the firm. As per above example, if the firm is able to earn only 10%. all the earnings will go in the hands of contributors of capital and nothing will be left in the business.

## Marginal Cost Of Capital

A company's marginal cost of capital (MCC) may increase as additional capital is raised, whereas returns to a company's investment opportunities are generally believed to decrease as the company makes additional investments, as represented by the investment opportunity schedule (IOS). The following graph demonstrate the relationship between cost of capital and investment returns. In the context of a company's investment decision, the optimal capital budget is that amount of capital raised and invested at which the marginal cost of capital is equal to the marginal return from investing. In other words, the optimal capital budget occurs when the marginal cost of capital intersects with the investment opportunity schedule.

The relation between the MCC and the Investment opportunity schedule (IOS) provides a broad picture of the basic decision-making problem of a company. However, we are often interested in valuing an individual project or even a portion of a company, such as a division or product line. In these applications, we are interested in the cost of capital for the project, product, or division as opposed to the cost of capital for the company overall.

## Project Cost Of Capital

The cost of capital in these applications should reflect the riskiness of the future cash flows of the project, product, or division. For an average-risk project, the opportunity cost of capital is the company's WACC. If the systematic risk of the project is above or below average relative to the company's current portfolio of projects, an upward or downward adjustment, respectively, is made to the company's WACC. Companies may take an ad hoc or a systematic approach to making such adjustments.

The WACC or MCC corresponding to the average risk of the company, adjusted appropriately for the risk of a given project, plays a role in capital budgeting decision making based on the net present value (NPV) of that project. NPV is the present value of all the project cash flows. It is useful to think of it as the difference between the present value of the cash inflows, discounted at the opportunity cost of capital applicable to the specific project, and the present value of the cash outflows, discounted using that same opportunity cost of capital.

*NPV =Present value of inflows - Present value of outflows*

If we choose to use the company's WACC in the calculation of the NPV of a project, we are assuming that the project:

- has the same risk as the average-risk project of the company, and
- will have a constant target capital structure throughout its useful life

These may not be realistic or appropriate assumptions and are potential drawbacks to using the company's WACC in valuing projects. However, alternative approaches are subject to drawbacks as well, and the approach has wider acceptance.

## Marginal Cost Of Capital And Asset Valuation

For the analyst, the second key use of the marginal cost of capital is in security valuation using any one of several discounted cash flow valuation models available. For a particular valuation model, if these cash flows are cash flows to the company's suppliers of capital, the analyst uses the weighted average cost of capital of the company in the valuation. If these cash flows are strictly those belonging to the company's owners, such as the free cash flow to equity, or dividends, the analyst uses the cost of equity capital to find the present value of these flows.

## Historical cost

In <u>accounting</u> under the traditional historical cost paradigm, **historical cost** is the original nominal monetary value of an economic item.[1] Historical cost is based on the stable measuring unit assumption. In some circumstances, <u>assets</u> and liabilities may be shown at their historical cost, as if there had been no change in value since the date of acquisition. The <u>balance sheet</u> value of the item may therefore differ from the real value.

While historical cost is criticised for its inaccuracy (deviation from real value), it remains in use in most accounting systems during low and high inflation and deflation. During hyperinflation, International Financial Reporting Standards require financial capital maintenance in units of constant purchasing power in terms of the monthly CPI as set out in IAS 29 Financial Reporting in Hyperinflationary Economies. Various corrections to historical cost are used, many of which require the use of management judgment and may be difficult to verify. The trend in most accounting standards is a move to more accurate reflection of the fair or market value, although the historical cost principle remains in use, particularly for assets of little importance.

Depreciation affects the carrying value of an asset on the balance sheet. The historical cost will equal the carrying value if there has been no change recorded in the value of the asset since acquisition. Improvements may be added to the cost basis of an asset.

Historical cost does not generally reflect current market valuation. Alternative measurement bases to the historical cost measurement basis, which may be applied for some types of assets for which market values are readily available, require that the carrying value of an asset (or liability) be updated to the market price (mark-to-market valuation) or some other estimate of value that better approximates the real value. Accounting standards may also have different methods required or allowed (even for different types of balance sheet variable real value non-monetary assets or liabilities) as to how the resultant change in value of an asset or liability is recorded, as a part of income or as a direct change to shareholders' equity.

**Importance of Cost of Capital**

The cost of capital is very important concept in the financial decision making. Cost of capital is the measurement of the sacrifice made by investors in order to invest with a view to get a fair return in future on his investments as a reward for the postponement of his present needs. On the other hand from the point of view of the firm using the capital, cost of capital is the price paid to the investor for the use of capital provided by him. Thus, cost of capital is reward for the use of capital. The progressive management always likes to consider the importance cost of capital while takingfinancial decisions as it's very relevant in the following spheres:

1.    Designing the capital structure: The cost of capital is the significant factor in designing a balanced and optimal capital structure of a firm. While designing it, the management has to consider the objective of maximizing the value of the firm and minimizing cost of capital. Comparing the various specific costs of different sources of capital, the financial manager can select the best and the most economical source of finance and can designed a sound andbalanced capital structure.

2.    Capital budgeting decisions: The cost of capital sources as a very useful tool in the process of making capital budgeting decisions. Acceptance or rejection of any investment proposal depends upon the cost of capital. A proposal shall not be accepted till its rate of return is greater than the cost of capital. In various methods of discounted cash flows of capital budgeting, cost of capital measured the financial performance

and determines acceptability of all investment proposals by discounting the cash flows.

3. Comparative study of sources of financing: There are various sources of financing a project. Out of these, which source should be used at a particular point of time is to be decided bycomparing costs of different sources of financing. The source which bears the minimum cost of capital would be selected. Although cost of capital is an important factor in such decisions, but equally important are the considerations of retaining control and of avoiding risks.

4. Evaluations of financial performance: Cost of capital can be used to evaluate the financial performance of the capital projects. Such as evaluations can be done by comparing actual profitability of the project undertaken with the actual cost of capital of funds raise to finance the project. If the actual profitability of the project is more than the actual cost of capital, the performance can be evaluated as satisfactory.

5. Knowledge of firms expected income and inherent risks: Investors can know the firms expected income and risks inherent there in by cost of capital. If a firms cost of capital is high, it means the firms present rate of earnings is less, risk is more and capital structure is imbalanced, in such situations, investors expect higher rate of return.

6.  Financing and Dividend Decisions: The concept of capital can be conveniently employed as a tool in making other important financial decisions. On the basis, decisions can be taken regarding dividend policy, capitalization of profits and selections of sources of working capital.

In sum, the importance of cost of capital is that it is used to evaluate new project of company and allows the calculations to be easy so that it has minimum return that investor expect for providing investment to the company.

**The Weighted Average Cost of Capital :**

What Does "Cost of Capital" Mean? "Cost of capital" is defined as "the opportunity cost of all capital invested in an enterprise."

**Let's dissect this definition:**

Opportunity cost is what you give up as a consequence of your decision to use a scarce resource in a particular way. All capital invested is the total amount of cash invested into a business. In an enterprise this refers to the fact that we are measuring the opportunity cost of all sources of capital which include debt and equity.

How Do We Calculate a Company's Weighted Average Cost of Capital? We calculate a company's weighted average cost of capital using a 3 step process:

1. Cost of capital components. First, we calculate or infer the cost of each kind of capital that the enterprise uses, namely debt and equity. A. Debt capital. The cost of debt capital is equivalent to actual or imputed interest rate on the company's debt, adjusted for the tax-deductibility of interest expenses. Specifically: The after-tax cost of debt-capital = The Yield-to-Maturity on long-term debt x (1 minus the marginal tax rate in %) We enter the marginal corporate tax rate in the worksheet "WACC." B. Equity capital. Equity shareholders, unlike debt holders, do not demand an explicit return on their capital. However, equity shareholders do face an implicit opportunity cost for investing in a specific company, because they could invest in an alternative company with a similar risk profile. Thus, we infer the opportunity cost of equity capital. We can do this by using the "Capital Asset Pricing Model" (CAPM). This model says that equity shareholders demand a minimum rate of return equal to the return from a risk-free investment plus a return for bearing extra risk. This extra risk is often called the "equity risk premium", and is equivalent to the risk premium of the market as a whole times a multiplier--called "beta"--that measures how risky a specific security is relative to the total market. Thus, the cost of equity capital = Risk-Free Rate + (Beta times Market Risk Premium).

2. Capital structure. Next, we calculate the proportion that debt and equity capital contribute to the entire enterprise, using the

market values of total debt and equity to reflect the investments on which those investors expect to earn a minimum return.

3. Weighting the components. Finally, we weight the cost of each kind of capital by the proportion that each contributes to the entire capital structure. This gives us the Weighted Average Cost of Capital (WACC), the average cost of each dollar of cash employed in the business.

## CAPITAL BUDGETING :

### Capital Budgeting Definition

Capital budgeting is the planning of long-term corporate financial projects relating to investments funded through and affecting the firm's capital structure. Management must allocate the firm's limited resources between competing opportunities (projects), which is one of the main focuses of capital budgeting. [2] Capital budgeting is also concerned with the setting of criteria about which projects should receive investment funding to increase the value of the firm, and whether to finance that investment with equity or debt capital. Investments should be made on the basis of value-added to the future of the corporation. Capital budgeting projects may include a wide variety of different types of investments, including but not limited to, expansion policies, or mergers and acquisitions. When no such value can be added through the capital budgeting process and excess cash surplus exists and is not needed, then management is expected to pay out some or all of those surplus earnings in the form of cash dividends or to repurchase the company's stock through a share buyback program.

Choosing between capital budgeting projects may be based upon several inter-related criteria. (1) Corporate management seeks to maximize the value of the firm by investing in projects which yield a positive net present value when valued using an appropriate discount rate in consideration of risk. (2) These projects must also be financed appropriately. (3) If no positive NPV projects exist and excess cash surplus is not needed to the firm, then financial theory suggests that management should return some or all of the excess cash to shareholders (i.e., distribution via dividends).

Capital budgeting involves allocating the firm's capital resources between competing project and investments. Each potential project's value should be estimated using adiscounted cash flow (DCF) valuation, to find its net present value (NPV). (First applied to Corporate Finance by Joel Dean in 1951.) This valuation requires estimating the size and timing of all the incremental cash flows from the project. (These future cash highest NPV(GE).) The NPV is greatly affected by the discount rate, so selecting the proper rate—sometimes called the *hurdle rate*—is critical to making the right decision. The hurdle rate is the Minimum acceptable rate of return on an investment. This should reflect the riskiness of the investment, typically measured by the volatility of cash flows, and must take into account the financing mix. Managers may use models such as the CAPM or the APT to estimate a discount rate appropriate for each particular project, and use the weighted average cost of capital (*WACC*) to reflect the financing mix selected. A common practice in choosing a discount rate for a project is to apply a WACC that applies to the entire firm, but a higher discount rate may be more appropriate when a project's risk is higher than the risk of the firm as a whole.

Ideally, businesses should pursue all projects and opportunities that enhance shareholder value. However, because the amount of capital available at any given time for new projects is limited, management needs to use capital budgeting techniques to determine which projects will yield the most return over an applicable period of time.

## CAPITAL BUDGETING TECHNIQUES

## INTRODUCTION

Any investment decision depends upon the decision rule that is applied under circumstances. However, the decision rule itself considers following inputs.

The effectiveness of the decision rule depends on how

these three factors have been properly assessed. Estimation of cash flows require immense understanding of the project before it is implemented; particularly macro and micro view of the economy, polity and the company. Project life is very important, otherwise it will change the entire perspective of the project. So great care is required to be observed for estimating the project life. Cost of capital is being considered as discounting factor which has undergone a change over the years. Cost of capital has different connotations in different economic philosophies. Particularly, India has undergone a change in its economic ideology from a closedeconomy to open-economy. Hence determination of cost of capital

## Net Present Value (NPV)

Net present value is the present value of net cash inflows generated by a project including salvage value, if any, less the initial investment on the project. It is one of the most reliable measures used in capital budgeting because it accounts for time value of money by using discounted cash inflows. Before calculating NPV, a target rate of return is set which is used to discount the net cash inflows from a project. Net cash inflow equals total cash inflow during a period less the expenses directly incurred on generating the cash inflow.

## Payback Period

Payback period is the time in which the initial cash outflow of an investment is expected to be recovered from the cash inflows generated by the investment. It is one of the simplest investment appraisal techniques.

Formula

The formula to calculate payback period of a project depends on whether the cash flow per period from the project is even or uneven. In case they are even, the formula to calculate payback period is:

Payback Period =    Initial Investment

Cash Inflow per Period

When cash inflows are uneven, we need to calculate the cumulative net cash flow for each period and then use the following formula for payback period:

Payback Period = A + B + C

In the above formula,

A is the last period with a negative cumulative cash flow;

B is the absolute value of cumulative cash flow at the end of the period A;

C is the total cash flow during the period after A

Advantages and Disadvantages

Advantages of payback period are:

1. Payback period is very simple to calculate.

2. It can be a measure of risk inherent in a project. Since cash flows that occur later in a project's life are considered more uncertain, payback period provides an indication of how certain the project cash inflows are.

3. For companies facing liquidity problems, it provides a good ranking of projects that would return money early.

Disadvantages of payback period are:

1. Payback period does not take into account the time value of money which is a serious drawback since it can lead to wrong decisions. A variation of payback method that attempts to remove this drawback is calleddiscounted payback period method.

2. It does not take into account, the cash flows that occur after the payback period.

Profitability Index

Profitability index is an investment appraisal technique calculated by dividing the present value of future cash flows of a project by the initial investment required for the project.

Formula:

Profitability Index

= Present Value of Future Cash Flows

Initial Investment Required

$$= 1 + \text{ Net Present Value}$$

Initial Investment Required

Explanation:

Profitability index is actually a modification of the net present value method. While present value is an absolute measure (i.e. it gives as the total dollar figure for a project), the profibality index is a relative measure (i.e. it gives as the figure as a ratio).

## AVERAGE RATE OF RETURN METHOD

1. TOTAL NET RETURN METHOD

2. RATE OF RETURN METHOD

3. AVERAGE RATE OF RETURN METHOD

(a) Pay Back Period (PBP) (b) Accounting Rate Of Return (ARR) 26 2.2.2 Discounted Cash Flow Criteria: - (a) Net Present Value (NPV) (b) Internal Rate of Return (IRR) (c) Profitability Index (PI) 2.2.1 Non-Discounted Cash Flow Criteria:

These are also known as traditional techniques: (a) Pay Back Period (PBP) : The pay back period (PBP) is the traditional method of capital budgeting. It is the simplest and perhaps, the most widely used quantitative method for appraising capital expenditure decision. Meaning: It is the number of years required to recover the original cash outlay invested in a project. Methods to compute PBP: There are two methods of calculating the PBP. (a) The first method can be applied when the CFAT is uniform. In such a situation the initial cost of the investment is divided by the constant annual cash flow,

Decision Rule: The PBP can be used as a decision criterion to select investment proposal. If the PBP is less than the maximum acceptable payback period, accept the project. If the PBP is greater than the maximum acceptable payback period, reject the project. This technique can be used to compare actual pay back with a standard pay back set up by the management in terms of the maximum period during which the initial investment must be recovered. The standard PBP is determined by management subjectively on the basis of a number of factors such as the type of project, the perceived risk of the project etc. PBP can be even used for ranking mutually exclusive projects. The projects may be ranked according to the length of PBP and the project with the shortest PBP will be selected.

Merits: 1. It is simple both in concept and application and easy to calculate. 2. It is a cost effective method which does not require much of the time of finance executives as well as the use of computers. 28 3. It is a method for dealing with risk. It favours projects which generates substantial cash inflows in earlier years and discriminates against projects which brings substantial inflows in later years . Thus PBP method is useful in weeding out risky projects. 4. This is a method of liquidity. It emphasizes selecting a project with the early recovery of the investment.

Demerits: 1. It fails to consider the time value of money. Cash inflows, in pay back calculations, are simply added without discounting. This violates the most basic principles of financial analysis that stipulates the cash flows occurring at different points of time can be added or subtracted only after suitable compounding/ discounting. 2. It ignores cash flows beyond PBP. This leads to reject projects that generate substantial inflows in later years. 3. It is a measure of projects capital recovery, not profitability so this can not be used as the only method of accepting or rejecting a project. The organization need to use some other method also which takes into account profitability of the project. 4. The projects are not getting preference as per their cash flow pattern. It gives equal weightage to the projects if their PBP is same but their pattern is different. 5. There is no logical base to decide standard PBP of the organization it is generally a subjective decision. 6. It is not consistent with the objective of shareholders' wealth maximization. The PBP of the projects will not affect the market price of equity shares. Uses:

The PBP can be gainfully employed under the following circumstances. 1. The PB method may be useful for the firms suffering from a liquidity crisis. 30 2. It is very useful for those firms which emphasizes on short run earning performance rather than its long term growth. 3. The reciprocal of PBP is a good approximation of IRR which otherwise requires trial & error approach. Payback Reciprocal and the Rate of Return: Payback is considered a good approximation of the rate of return under following two conditions. 1. The life of the project is too large or at least twice the pay back period. 2. The project generates constant annual cash inflow. Though pay back reciprocal is a useful way to estimate the project's IRR but the major limitation of it is all investment project does not satisfy the conditions on which this method is based. When the useful life of the project is not at least twice the PBP, it will always exceed the rate of return. Similarly, if the project is not yielding constant CFAT it can not be used as an approximation of the rate of return.2 Discounted Payback Period: One of the major limitations of PBP method is that it does not take into consideration time value of money. This problem can be solved if we discount the cash flows and then calculate the PBP. Thus, discounted payback period is the number of years taken in recovering the investment outlay on the present value basis.

(b) Accounting/Average Rate of Return (ARR): This method is also known as the return on investment (ROI), return on capital employed (ROCE) and is using accounting information rather than cash flow. Meaning: The ARR is the ratio of the average after tax profit divided by the average investment. Method to compute ARR: There are a number of alternative methods for calculating ARR. The most common method of computing ARR is using the following formula:

$$ARR = \underline{\text{Average Annual profit After Tax}} \quad X\ 100$$

$$\text{Average investment}$$

Decision Rule: The ARR can be used as a decision criterion to select investment proposal. If the ARR is higher than the minimum rate established by the management, accept the project. If the ARR is less than the minimum rate established by the management, reject the project. 33 The ranking method can also be used to select or reject the proposal using ARR. It will rank a project number one if it has highest ARR and lowest rank would be given to the project with lowest ARR.

Merits: 1. It is simple to calculate. 2. It is based on accounting information which is readily available and familiar to businessman. 3. It considers benefit over entire life of the project.

Demerits: 1. It is based upon accounting profit, not cash flow in evaluating projects. 2. It does not take into consideration time value of money so benefits in the earlier years or later years cannot be valued at par. 3. This method does not take into consideration any benefits which can accrue to the firm from the sale or abandonment of equipment which is replaced by a new investment. ARR does not make any adjustment in this regard to determine the level of average investments. 4. Though it takes into account all years income but it is averaging out the profit. 5. The firm compares any project's ARR with the one which is arbitrarily decided by management generally based on the firm's current return on assets. Due to this yardstick sometimes super normal growth firm's reject profitable projects if it's ARR is less than the firm's current earnings. Use: The ARR can better be used as performance evaluation measure and control devise but it is not advisable to use as a decision making criterion for capital expenditures of the firm as it is not using cash flow information. 34 2.2.2 Discounted Cash Flow Criteria: These are also known as modern or time adjusted techniques because all these techniques take into consideration time value of money.

## (a) Net Present Value (NPV):

The net present value is one of the discounted cash flow or time-adjusted technique. It recognizes that cash flow streams at different time period differs in value and can be computed only when they are expressed in terms of common denominator i.e. present value. Meaning: The NPV is the difference between the present value of future cash inflows and the present value of the initial outlay, discounted at the firm's cost of capital. The procedure for determining the present values consists of two stages. The first stage involves determination of an appropriate discount rate. With the discount rate so selected, the cash flow streams are converted into present values in the second stage.

Method to compute NPV: The important steps for calculating NPV are given below3 . 1. Cash flows of the investment project should be forecasted based on realistic assumptions. These cash flows are the incremental cash inflow after taxes and are inclusive of depreciation (CFAT) which is assumed to be received at the end of each year. CFAT should take into account salvage value and working capital released at the end. 2. Appropriate discount rate should be identified to discount the forecasted cash flows. The appropriate discount rate is the firm's opportunity cost of capital 3 ibid, pg. 143 35 which is equal to the required rate of return expected by investors on investments of equivalent risk. 3. Present value (PV) of cash flows should be calculated using opportunity cost of capital as the discount rate. 4. NPV should be found out by subtracting present value of cash outflows from present value of cash inflows. The project should be accepted if NPV is positive (i.e. NPV >0) The NPV can be calculated with the help of equation.

NPV = Present value of cash inflows – Initial investment ( ) ( ) ( ) C K A K A K A W n n − + + + + + + = 1 ....... 1 1 2 2 1 1 ( ) $\sum$ = − + = n t t C K t A NPV 1 1 OR NPV = ( ) 0 1 CF PVIF , CF n t $\sum$ t × k t − = Where, A1,A2 ... represent the stream of benefits expected to occur if a course of action is adopted, C is the cost of that action & K is the appropriate discount rate to measure the quality of A's. W is the NPV or, wealth which is the difference between the present worth of the stream of benefits and the initial cost. CFt is the cash flow for t period PVIF is the present value interest factor 36 Decision Rule: The present value method can be used as an accept-reject criterion. The present value of the future cash streams or inflows would be compared with present value of outlays. The present value outlays are the same as the initial investment. If the NPV is greater than 0, accept the project. If the NPV is less than 0, reject the project. Symbolically, accept-reject criterion can be shown as below: PV > C → Accept [NPV > 0] PV < C → Reject [NPV < 0] Where, PV is present value of inflows and C is the outlays This method can be used to select between mutually exclusive projects also. Using NPV the project with the highest positive NPV would be ranked first and that project would be selected. The market value of the firm's share would increase if projects with positive NPVs are accepted.4 For example, Calculate NPV for a Project X initially costing Rs. 250000. It has 10% cost of capital. It generates following cash flows: 4 Van Horne, J.C., Financial Management and Policy, Prentice-Hall of India, 1974, p.74 37 Year Cash flows PV @ 10% PV 1 90000 0.909 81810 2 80000 0.826 66080 3 70000 0.751 52570 4 60000 0.683 40980 5 50000 0.621 31050 Less: ΣPV 272490 NCO 250000 NPV( Rs.) 22490 As the project has positive NPV, i.e. present value of cash inflows is greater than the cash outlays, it should be accepted. Merits: This method is considered as the most appropriate measure of profitability due to following virtues. 1. It explicitly recognizes the time value of money. 2. It takes into account all the years cash flows arising out of the project over its useful life. 3. It is an absolute measure of profitability. 4. A changing discount rate can be built into NPV calculation. This feature becomes important as this rate normally changes because the longer the time span, the lower the value of money & higher the discount rate. 5 5 Jain P K & Khan M Y, Financial Management (4th ed),Tata McGraw-Hill Publishing Company Ltd, pg 10.25 38 5. This is the only method which satisfies the value-additivity principle. It gives output in terms of absolute amount so the NPVs of the projects can be added which is not possible with other methods. For example, NPV (X+Y) = NPV (X) + NPV (Y). Thus, if we know the NPV of all project undertaken by the firm, it is possible to calculate the overall value of the firm. 6 6. It is always consistent with the firm's goal of shareholders wealth maximization. Demerits: 1. This method requires estimation of cash flows which is very difficult due to uncertainties existing in business world due to so many uncontrollable environmental factors. 2. It requires the calculation of the required rate of return to discount the cash flows. The discount rate is the most important element used in the calculation of the present values because different discount rates will give different present values. The relative desirability of the proposal will change with a change in the discount rate.7 3. When projects under consideration are mutually exclusive, it may not give dependable results if the projects are having unequal lives, different cash flow pattern, different cash outlay etc. 4. It does not explicitly deal with uncertainty when valuing the project and the extent of management's flexibility to respond to uncertainty over the life of the project.8 5. It ignores the value of creating options. Sometimes an investment that appears uneconomical when viewed in isolation may, in fact, create options that enable the firm to undertake other investments in the future should market conditions turn 6 Pandey I M, Financial Management, Vikas Publishing House Pvt Ltd, p.145 7 op.cit. 8 Madhani Pankaj M, RO-Based Capital Budgeting: A Dynamic Approach in New Economy, The ICFAI Journal of Applied Finance, November 2008, Vol. 14, No. 11, pg 48-67 39 favourable. By not accounting properly for the options that investments in emerging technology may yield, naive NPV analysis can lead firms to invest too little.9 Use: NPV is very much in use capital budgeting practice being a true profitability measure.

(b) Profitability Index (PI): Profitability Index (PI) or Benefit-cost ratio (B/C) is similar to the NPV approach. PI approach measures the present value of returns per rupee invested. It is observed in shortcoming of NPV that, being an absolute measure, it is not a reliable method to evaluate projects requiring different initial investments. The PI method provides solution to this kind of problem.

Meaning: It is a relative measure and can be defined as the ratio which is obtained by dividing the present value of future cash inflows by the present value of cash outlays.